Wherever I Am, I'm Fine

Wherever I Am, I'm Fine

Letters About Living While Dying

Catherine Royce

To order additional copies of this book, contact:
Xlibris Corporation
1-888-795-4274
www.Xlibris.com
Orders@Xlibris.com
52758

For My Beloveds

FOREWORD

The first time I heard the word ALS I was nine years old, some 60 years ago. I was watching a movie called "Pride of the Yankees, the life story of Lou Gehrig." I was profoundly moved by Gehrig's courage as he stood in front of an enormous cluster of microphones at Yankee Stadium and spoke to millions of people all over the world, knowing that ALS not only had robbed him of his immortal baseball skills but had sentenced him to death. Everyone present that day held his or her breath as he spoke:

"Today," he said, "I consider myself to be the luckiest man on the face of the earth."

Catherine Royce has ALS, and has been told by her medical support team that there is no cure. Every moment, she has been forced to watch her life relentlessly draining out of her.

"And yet," Catherine says, "I always have a choice."

She goes on to say: "Everyday I choose not only how I will live, but if I will live. I have no particular religious mandate that forbids contemplating a shorter life, an action that would deny this disease its ultimate expression. But this is where my belief in choice truly finds its power. I can choose to see ALS as nothing more than a death sentence, or I can choose to see it as an invitation—an opportunity to learn who I truly am."

Where does such incredible wisdom and courage come from?

I have known Catherine and her family for close to 15 years. We are both part of a worldwide meditation community known as Siddha Yoga. The practice of meditation, for the past 30 years, has been the source of inspiration, wisdom and courage that has continuously guided Catherine's beautiful life.

Through the practices of contemplation and meditation, Catherine has been able to stay connected to the innermost part of her being, the ultimate source of her tremendous insight and love, and the place where she has been able to access the peace that has helped her to transcend her pain and fear. Having had to face ALS head-on, Catherine has had to call on the power of her deepest Self more profoundly than ever before. She writes:

"So far I have discovered many unique things, but one stands out above the rest. I have discovered in myself an ability to recognize, give, and receive caring in a way far deeper than anything in my life before. Previously, I would have assumed living with ALS meant a life of hardship and isolation. Instead, because I believe that I always have a choice, I opened myself to other possibilities. And now the very thing that at first seemed so abhorrent has graced my life with unaccustomed sweetness. It was always there. Only now I have chosen to see it."

Catherine's message—"I Always have a choice"—is truly an invocation to us all. Knowing that she is living her life with great conviction and joy, while staring into the eyes of death each moment, speaks loudly of what the human spirit is capable of no matter what the outer circumstances might be. She points us to the profound experience of true Freedom: the certain knowledge that even though death eventually approaches everyone of us, and our bodies ultimately dissolve, there is a part of us that remains, and that our life, after all, is everlasting.

With much love and respect,
Alan Gompers

Alan Gompers has been practicing and teaching meditation for the past 30 years. He is the author of the memoir *Maximum Security: The True Meaning of Freedom.*

INTRODUCTION

It was in the summer of 2004—just over four years ago as I write this—that our friend and neighbor Catherine Royce called with an ominous message: "I have something important to tell you." It had been awhile since we'd gotten together. We sat around the kitchen table and talked about our children, what was going on in our lives, tip-toeing around the mystery. Finally Catherine came out with it: "I have ALS."

My wife Jean and I knew all too well what this meant. ALS interrupted the career of a former student of hers, an English professor at a small Midwestern college. To be near his parents, Phil Simmons and his family moved to a small town in New Hampshire that we visit often. We called on Phil regularly, talked at length, and read his beautifully-crafted essays, collected in a book called *Learning to Fall*. I reported for NPR on the way the community rallied to support Phil and his family, enabling him to stay at home through the long trajectory of his illness. Eventually we grieved Phil's loss. So at Catherine's news, our hearts sank.

Since then, ALS has done to Catherine, her family and friends what it so inexorably does to many thousands of others. At any given time, the ALS Association estimates about 30,000 Americans are in various stages of the disease. That makes it rare, striking one in

100,000 people, compared to one in 760 for multiple sclerosis and one in 61 for Alzheimers. The visibility of ALS has risen in recent years. Just today, when I mentioned Catherine's situation to a woman I know, her response was: "Isn't ALS becoming more common?" Fortunately, there's no evidence that's true. But it is a good thing that ALS is becoming better known, for reasons I'll talk about in a moment.

Rare though it is, ALS is one of the cruelest diseases. Typically its victims, like Catherine and Phil, are in the prime of life. There's usually no family history or apparent reason why they should suddenly have the symptoms of a neuromuscular disease—tripping, dropping things, fumbling with keys, muscle cramps and twitches.

One other distinguishing feature is both a blessing and a curse; unlike other neurodegenerative diseases, ALS patients typically maintain normal or near-normal cognitive function as their bodies wither and fail. Phil Simmons used to say, with mordant humor, "ALS gives you a front-row seat on your own demise."

Because this is so, however, some ALS patients have produced remarkably eloquent meditations on what it means to be alive. This is such a collection. Catherine has already illuminated the lives of many people with her rigorous, open-hearted and relentlessly candid meditations on living with, and despite, ALS. Millions heard one of her essays, "I Believe I Always Have a Choice," as part of NPR's *This I Believe* series.

This testimony is important. Clearly, it's been important to her, her family, her many friends, her caregivers. But it's important in a more public way.

Until fairly recently, most people knew amyotrophic lateral sclerosis as the disease that ended Lou Gehrig's record-breaking baseball career in 1939. Now most people know ALS as a disease that can strike close to home—somebody they know, or the friend of a friend. Partly that's because of writing by and about the valiant people who have no choice but to cope with the disease. Dr. Merit Cudkowicz, a Massachusetts General Hospital doctor who is Catherine's neurologist, says this has had an effect.

"What we've found is that as people have been paying more attention to this illness, we're taking better care of these patients," Dr. Cudkowicz told me. "And survival has improved in the last decade."

That's not because of any medical breakthrough. The available medication, when it helps at all, may extend life by about 10 percent. No, the improvement has come about, first, through a change in the sense of futility that used to envelope both ALS patients and their caregivers; and second, from the application of medical common sense.

Since ALS patients develop problems swallowing, their nutrition declines and they lose weight—compromising energy and setting them up for painful and easily infected pressure ulcers. But a more proactive stance is leading some practitioners to intervene—implanting tubes so nutrition can be delivered directly to the stomach—before such severe weight loss. Since ALS patients gradually lose strength in the muscles of breathing, doctors earlier and more often prescribe breathing support with a device that delivers puffs of oxygen into the nose. That prevents the nighttime dips in blood-oxygen levels that ALS patients often experience, compromising sleep and stealing energy.

At the best ALS treatment centers, teams of doctors, respiratory therapists, speech and "swallow therapists," physical therapists, nurse practitioners, and social workers try to maintain function, manage pain, and otherwise optimize care. This is not cheap. Dr. Cudkowicz says the equipment to extend life and mobility costs at least $20,000, and many insurers won't pay. Total medical costs run around $100,000 a year.

Disability determinations, triggering Medicare coverage for some of these expenses, are rife with delay and catch-22s—as Catherine has found. Some ALS patients, like Catherine, are lucky to have friends who help sustain a semblance of normal, uninstitutionalized life . . . until they get overwhelmed. Many, Dr. Cudkowicz says, "are not so blessed."

Still, there are signs of change. In September, 2008, the Department of Veterans Affairs decided to grant military veterans with ALS full health and disability benefits, on the presumption that their disease is service-connected, wherever they served. That's based on studies showing that veterans are almost twice as likely to develop ALS as the general population, for reasons that are still unclear.

The same month, Congress passed legislation to set up a national registry of patients with ALS. Eventually that should help researchers discover commonalities among people with the disease—patterns that can point the way toward risk factors and ultimately causes.

Only about one in five ALS patients has a family history of the disease, a pattern that has led scientists to a defect in a gene called SOD1. People who inherit the defective gene have a 50/50 chance of getting ALS. Other research suggests that athletes, in particular endurance athletes such as marathoners, have about twice the risk of ALS.

But 80 percent of ALS cases have no apparent risk factors. Scientists are pursuing some tantalizing clues. One idea is that people who get ALS suffer from too much glutamate, a chemical that transmits signals between certain nerve cells. It turns out autopsies of people who died from ALS show most of them lack a molecule that clears glutamate. That would allow glutamate to build up in the nervous system, essentially burning out nerve cells from glutamate toxicity. Researchers are looking for drugs to prevent glutamate buildup or inhibit glutamate release.

Another research lead involves mitochondria, the energy powerhouses within each cell. Some researchers think ALS patients have a defect that gums up mitochondrial metabolism. Figuring out how, as with the glutamate hypothesis, could give doctors a way of diagnosing ALS early and treating with drugs to compensate.

It's not going to happen fast. But ALS is a lively area of research at last, and scientists have tools they never had before. The pace of progress will depend in large part on how visible ALS remains. That's one reason why books like this are important.

But of course, that's not remotely why Catherine Royce wrote these letters to her "dear ones." In fact, this book is not really about ALS at all. It's about the triumph of the human spirit.

Richard Knox
Science Correspondent
National Public Radio

In late 2004 and early 2005, a wide circle of friends and family contributed enough funds to enable Catherine to travel to India for five weeks of treatment at an ayurvedic medical center in Nagpur. A friend established a website to facilitate contributions. Catherine used the website to post updates about her trip, and continued the letters when she returned home to Boston.

This book is a compilation of those letters. Numerous Sanskrit words and ayurvedic medical terms are defined in parentheses, and background information has been inserted where necessary.

PROLOGUE

I first became aware of symptoms of muscle weakening and cramping in my left hand and forearm in the late summer of 2001. By the summer of 2003, loss of muscle mass in my left hand was notable. Consultations with two neurologists in Boston and the results of two EMG's confirmed a diagnosis of ALS in October 2003. I was given a 10-year trajectory. Since then, the weakness, cramping and muscle deterioration have spread.

Today, I notice symptoms in my lower left arm and hand, my left thigh, calf and foot, and my right foot and calf. Reflexes in both ankles, both knees, both wrists and both elbows are what is called "brisk." I also notice that my voice tires more easily. My breathing and swallowing are tested regularly and continue to be normal.

Over the past year and a half, I have consulted with homeopaths, holistic doctors, traditional Chinese doctors, acupuncturists, cranio-sacral therapists, and have investigated other non-traditional modalities. I was also involved in an ALS drug trial through my neurologist at Massachusetts General Hospital. The advantage to the drug trial was that my symptoms were evaluated once a month, rather than the usual three months, so I had a better sense of what was going on. The bad news was that the drug was completely ineffective, as was everything else I looked into.

In the early fall of 2004, I was introduced to ayurvedic medicine, the traditional herbal medicine of India. In December, I flew to Albuquerque to consult with Dr. Sunil Joshi. In conjunction with one of his students in Boston, he put me on a regimen of herbs, twice-weekly massage, meditation, restricted diet and specific yoga postures. His approach was, at first, very conservative. He told me he would monitor my progress through his student. If my response to the regimen was negligible, he would propose a moderate, at-home treatment or no treatment at all. If my response was measurable, the next step would be a five-week panchakarma protocol (traditional cleansing therapies) *in India at his clinic. Fortunately, my body responded with immediate, significant enthusiasm. Most notably, my vata* (one of the humors) *which had been very high, began to drop precipitously.*

—Catherine Royce
from a paper presented at a conference on
ayurvedic medicine in Las Vegas, March, 2005

Part One

7 February 2005
Boston, Massachusetts

Hello, Dear Ones,

As I try to keep trip preparation anxiety and excitement under control (where does one end and the other begin?), I am writing to tell you all how wonderful you are. In a real sense, I've been preparing for this trip my entire life, but without your support I would not be getting on the plane for India tomorrow.

A few months ago, I had a dream. I don't remember the details, but I do remember the tag line. In the dream, I heard someone say to me "Whoever is with you now is along for the ride." So we're on a ride together, and I am so happy you're here.

Yesterday morning, I was meditating and having a little chat with God. She asked if I was worried about any aspect of the trip. I said I was a little nervous about the airport in Mumbai (I'll be arriving in the late evening and have about 10 hours before my next flight to Nagpur). I got an immediate response: "Look for me in the airport in Mumbai." So we shall see what form this takes!

So, here's what the next couple of days look like: I leave Boston tomorrow for JFK. JFK to Paris for a lay-over. Then Paris to Mumbai, arriving in Mumbai at 10pm. My flight to Nagpur leaves at 7:00 the next morning. I think I'll be there sometime late Wednesday evening, US East Coast time. Mukul Joshi, Dr. Joshi's brother, will meet me at the airport in Nagpur and bring me to the clinic. I've been corresponding with Mukul for the past couple of weeks and cannot wait to meet him—and everyone else, of course. For a sense of what the clinic's like, go to their website: *www.vinayakayurveda.com.*

Now, if I can just get all this stuff into one suitcase. How can I possibly be bringing so much? Actually, my Indian friends have counseled me well, and I am arriving well-supplied with gifts—bringing more than just my sparkling countenance.

My sparkling countenance will be back in touch again when I am in India. Bon Voyage to us all!

Love,
Catherine

12 February 2005
Nagpur, India

Dear Ones,

I'm here! How do I know? Well, first there was that 14-hour plane ride, which stopped for several hours in an airport that alleged to be Frankfurt (Surprise! Vee vent to Fraaankfoort, not Paree, but the airport looked like anywhere. My wheelchair escort was a Chinese woman from Shanghai.) In Frankfurt, I watched a hazy sunrise. I'm pretty sure the haziness was actual fog and not my mind. I also saw sunset in New York and followed by sunset somewhere over Turkey. So at least the sun still seemed to be turning on its axis.

Then there was the airport in Mumbai—now no one could make that up. No experience in the West could have prepared me for the sensory overload of the Mumbai airport (an experience years ago in the airport in Jakarta comes close). Fortunately, my wheelchair escort (Indian, this time—another clue that I was really here) knew all the angles and swiftly and surely steered me through immigration, baggage claim, customs, and out to the street. There, he deftly handed me over to the car the Hotel Leela had sent to pick me up. It was quite late at night and the flight was late. My escort even knew exactly where to suggest I give him his tip, as tipping porters in the airport is forbidden.

The Leela Hotel lived up to its name, I'm afraid. Though it is beautiful and has a solicitous staff, and though they sent a car to pick me up at the airport (I had a reservation, after all), they did not have a room for me. After sitting threateningly (or pathetically?) in the lobby for a long time (and refusing to disappear into the nearby lounge as they suggested), they apologized again and said they had a room if I didn't mind staying in their newly renovated handicapped accessible room. Were they kidding? Never mind. After a tutorial on how to get the lights to work, I slept soundly for four hours in a very comfy bed. So, do I know I'm in India now?

Before dawn I was heading back to another airport, the domestic one this time, for the flight to Nagpur. Everything seemed chaotic, though apparently only to me. Everyone else went about their business with conspicuous ease, so I attempted to do the same, though sleep deprivation was starting to addle my brain, English became the second and sometimes the third language.

Nagpur is beautiful, lots of trees, flowers, wide avenues, and—my final clue that I'm indeed in India—a complete absence of New England snow! Mukul Joshi, Dr. Joshi's brother, welcomed me at the airport and whisked me off across town to the clinic. Somehow, despite the lack of sleep, I was wide awake and absorbed all the sights. It was a beautiful day, warm with a cooling breeze. After about 20 minutes, we arrived at the clinic, which looks like the drawing on Dr. Joshi's website, except that it has near neighbors. Very near. But the clinic is beautiful—all green marble and white walls, immaculately clean. I was greeted immediately by Privin, Nilima, and Nita, three people who will figure prominently in my life here. Privin is the master of massage and application of certain medicines. Nilima is Dr. Joshi's nurse, and Nita keeps a watchful and compassionate eye on everything that happens in the clinic. They are all extraordinarily kind and handsome people. I was introduced as a friend of Kathy Curley's, whose name seems to have a lot of weight in these parts.

Mukul coordinated the rest of my day, apparently with the sole purpose of keeping me awake. He took me to my room and encouraged me to unpack. Then he encouraged me to explore my surroundings. The clinic has an open-air room on the roof that affords a view of the surrounding street and square. I sat up there for a while just watching the world go by. It was then that I knew with giddy certainty that I was in India.

When I came back downstairs, there was Mukul, who suggested that my room on the 2nd floor was too far from the dining and meditation halls. He wanted to move me to the first floor so I would have less stair climbing to do. There is a lift, but as the clinic (and all of this section of Nagpur, perhaps all of Nagpur) is without electricity every day between 9am and noon, stairs are still a necessity. So, everything was repacked and I moved to the new room. The rooms are spartan but comfortable, two beds (for when your husband comes, they assured me), two desks, a double closet, and a small table. The bathroom is basically a large shower that also contains a sink and toilet. Just as I finished unpacking again, there was Mukul. Was I hungry? Well, yes, I was. So he took me into the little dining hall and showed me the logistics of food distribution. It's ingenious. Each resident has a medium-sized thermos into which fits a stack of small covered metal bowls. Our names are on the lids (mine says "Chtherine"), and anytime after noon and again after around 6:00, we can come in and retrieve our meals, which are consumed communally around a large table. We are expected to serve and clean up after ourselves, which makes for an instant family atmosphere.

While I had been exploring, I ran into Dr. Joshi, who gave me a big hug, thanked me for coming, and suggested that if I was still awake at 5:00 that evening, he'd like to see me. Somehow, I managed to stay awake. So at 6:00, he invited me into his office and gave a consultation, a duplicate of the one he gave in December in Albuquerque. This consisted of a long period of listening to my pulses on both wrists, asking me questions, and taking copious notes. He checked my blood pressure, throat, abdomen, heart, tongue, and back. I told him about the extremely painful time I had had with my back during the previous month. He smiled sweetly and looked delighted. He noted the weight I had lost since I saw him last, and agreed it wasn't just because my hair is now much shorter. Again, delight. In fact, everything I told him seemed to bring a smile. Since I began on his regimen in December, the involuntary muscle twitching so characteristic of ALS seems to have mostly gone away.

As he had in December, he explained what his treatment is intended to do. I will try to do justice to his explanation, but I'm pretty sure I could not pass a quiz on Ayurveda 101 just yet. Ayurveda holds to the belief that the gut has its own specific nervous system. When the GI track isn't working properly, toxins accumulate in the system and it fails to work efficiently. Over time, this can result in compromises and failures in other parts of the body, especially in the brain and central nervous system. The goal of his treatment is to completely clean out my GI track and in so doing, stop whatever it is in my brain and nervous system that is causing my ALS symptoms. He stresses the transformative nature of this work on the physical as well as the spiritual level. So, while his treatment includes herbs, oils, diet and massage, it also includes twice daily meditation and hatha yoga. He believes that each area is critical to overall success and asked me to commit myself fully to both. When he finished, he assured me that now that I am here, I should not worry about anything. He and his staff will take care of me completely. He left me with a carefully designed regimen that includes, along with the diet, yoga and meditation, 12 different herbs that come in an assortment of powders, pills and liquids and a detailed schedule for their consumption. He then wished me *namaste** and sent me off to bed.

Yesterday morning, I began my treatments. At each step, the person working with me placed a hand on me and blessed me before beginning. In the morning, I had a long massage, designed to move my lymphatic fluids. This massage included copious amounts of special oil and covered every part of my body, even up my nose. At one point, Privin, who administers all the massages, also whacked the side of my head with a bean bag. I don't know why, but it didn't hurt. The massage is quick and very vigorous. For a small man, Privin is remarkably strong. After massage, he used a kind of steam wand to open my pores and encourage the oil to go more deeply into my body. Then he introduced me to the concept of *basti*. At this point anyone who is squeamish should skip down a paragraph because I promised you I would tell you all about my experience and *basti* is a critical component.

Now I'm a good WASP. I don't have bodily functions, and if I do, I sure don't talk about them, even to myself. But, ayurveda is all about the alimentary canal, so ultimately it's all about what happens (oh, how can I say this?) in the bowels, what goes in and, of course, what comes out. It's the "coming out" part that is so important, and a lot of time is spent encouraging things to come out and then examining and talking about them when they do. So, you can see I'm truly in my element here. Others of you in mid—life, may know the joys of sigmoidoscopy, if not colonoscopy, so you know the wonders of preparing the colon for, as they say in Hollywood, its close up. Well, *basti* is like the enema part of that preparation. Oh, joy! But actually, the one I had yesterday morning was nowhere near as wrenching as I remember the old Fleet enema to be. And what went in, did indeed, shortly come out. It gave new meaning to the expression: *Everything comes out well in the end.* I understand I will be doing a lot of *basti.* The other residents sit around at night and try to think up clever ways of describing this most basic of experiences. We sound a bit like seventh grade boys. What's wonderful is that before insertion, Privin asks permission to do it. I had to tell him: "I didn't come all this way to say no." He laughed, which he does easily and often. "I have to ask," he replied.

The next incident will have special meaning for followers of Siddha Yoga. As I was lying on the table in the midst of my treatment, a wonderful sound came through the window. It was a chorus of male voices chanting heartily. What they were chanting was unmistakable. It was the noon *arati.* I mentioned this to Privin and he said he thought someone in the neighborhood was having a *puja, a* religious ceremony.

In the afternoon, I had a sublime treatment whose name I can't remember. I lay on a table in a dark room while gentle music played. Privin put cool cloths over my eyes and encouraged me to empty my mind. Then he poured a steady stream of body-temperature oil over particular points on my forehead. After he had done this for a while, he gave my head a strong massage (and thanked me again for my short hair). Then he wrapped my face in a towel and instructed me to lie still for ten minutes. Of course, with a towel over my head, I couldn't see the clock, so I just spaced out for what seemed like a nice long time. For the rest of the day, I could have been standing next to someone wearing one of those t-shirts that says "I'm with stupid."

And how's the jet lag going? Well, I am writing this at 2:00 in the morning, but I'd say things are going well.

Love to you all,
Catherine

14 February 2005
Nagpur, India

Happy Valentines Day, everyone!

Being here is very much like being on retreat. I'll describe a typical day at the clinic. I wake up early, between 4:30 and 5:30. As I get used to the time change, my waking is later. At this hour of the morning, Nagpur is quiet, the air is cool, and the birds welcome the day. I begin my day by chanting the *Guru Gita*, followed by the first of my two daily mandated sessions of *pranayama* breathing and meditation.

Now, thanks to the intervention of Lisa and Frank who are in treatment here with me, I have access to my laptop. The adapter and converter that I had brought with me were wrong. But Lisa is a computer person and Frank is cheerfully determined. The two of them got what I needed and had my laptop up and running in a day.

I'll see Lisa and Frank in a few minutes when I walk down the hall to breakfast. During breakfast, Privin will come in and tell us all our treatment times for the morning. Mine has been around 9:30. So in a moment, I'll get cleaned up, put on the four dollar pants with the elephants along the cuff that I bought yesterday, and go in to eat a leisurely breakfast, in the company of the delightful people who are here with me.

In addition to Lisa and Frank, there is Valerie, who, like Lisa and Frank, is from New Mexico. The four of us have spent a great deal of time together, and they have been extraordinarily supportive. While everyone else is expected to serve themselves their own food and wash their own dishes, they have told me firmly that I am not allowed to. I'm guessing that's because my juggling of plates and crutches could result in food and broken crockery on the floor. I know that ultimately Anuja or Nita would come along and take care of it, but Frank usually steps in and dispatches everything with endearing enthusiasm.

Yesterday, Frank and Lisa showed me how to make my way down High Court Road for my first shopping trip. Bill, who is a doctor from Las Vegas, Angela, from England, and an Indian woman whose name I have not yet learned, round out our little family. Bill and Angela leave tomorrow and in the whirlwind of preparation for their departure, we have had limited opportunity to get to know each other.

On to the main events: the treatments. There are two a day, except Sunday when Privin actually takes the afternoon off, to please his wife, he says. A general description of the focus of my day accurately falls under the heading Process of Elimination (POE). The process is everything—good thing that I've always been a process person!

In the morning, Privin administers a very vigorous and oily massage. It alternates between being sublimely soothing and quite painful, especially when he works on my legs and feet. After the massage, as I noted, he passes a steam hose all over my skin to move the oil deeply into my body, aiding the POE. After the steaming, Privin washes my body with near-scalding water. When he asks if it's too hot and I say "a little," he says "Good."

It's quite a trick to get off the table when the massage is complete. I'm so oily and relaxed, it's a good thing there are grab bars to help me!

All this oily fun is designed to prepare for the next event. In a classic johnny—open at the back of course—I am escorted to the next room. There, Privin administers oil in specific places. The other day he used dough to create two craters on my back, one at the base of my neck and the other at the base of my spine. He poured warm oil into these reservoirs while I tried to empty my mind, as instructed.

After this pleasant experience is complete comes the absolute high point of the morning. Of couse, it's the *basti*. Because of Privin's good nature and his conviction that everything he does is for the absolute best healing, *basti* is bearable. What follows after the application of *basti* entirely depends on my body's reaction to that day's choice of basti herbs and oils. So far, for me, the immediate next step is a dash to the bathroom. See how basic this is? This clinic is one of the few places on earth I can imagine where the processing of the alimentary canal is acceptable dinner table conversation!

After the morning treatment, which lasts around an hour and a half, the middle of the day is mine. I write, sleep (this POE is hard work!), chat up the other residents, read, take a walk (it's still not too hot to walk in the middle of the day), check email (there's only one computer with internet access, so demand is high), sit on the roof and watch the wonder of the street scene below, or run errands.

Today, I want to find the post office, the bank, and a purveyor of phone calling cards. If I accomplish even one of those tasks, it will be a good day. On the other hand, the neighborhood monkey may decide to saunter by. He is a handsome and well-fed fellow, and all the westerners run to the window to see him. The Indians try to shoo him away. We are told he bites. If he shows up, ambition for all other activities falls away.

Later in the afternoon, there will be another treatment. These afternoon treatments are designed, I'm convinced, to make us all feel that despite the more unpleasant things we are subjecting ourselves to here, we are still fundamentally beautiful. So far, in the afternoons, we have been treated to eye treatments, facials and something called *shiradhara* (I'm probably misspelling that).

The eye treatments reintroduce the dough craters, which this time are shaped to form a rather fetching pair of glasses. Oil is then poured into the craters and we are strongly encouraged, well, *ordered* to open and close our eyes slowly for about 10 minutes. It's a very strange sensation. This is supposed to both improve visual acuity and mitigate dry eyes. A few hours after the treatment, the goo finally clears. I don't know that I'm seeing any better, but never mind. At one point during this treatment, the steam hose is brought out; I found the application of steam to my oily eyes a bit claustrophobic.

The facial is very vigorous and involves, what else, copious quantities of oil and then a mud mask. The scalp is also massaged, and the overall experience is very pleasant.

But *shiradhara* is by far my favorite. It's the one where a stream of warm oil is slowly poured over the forehead. Now I know its name. It encourages a sublime peacefulness.

This is my current day. The folks who have been here longer say that some elements may change as I go further into the POE. But I'm doing my best to stay in the present and not worry too much about what lies ahead.

I am just beginning day four of my treatment, so I can't say there's been a noticeable result just yet. One thing I am aware of is that after the morning massages, my legs feel much looser and more "awake." They feel stronger.

There were legions of weddings over the past weekend, so the air around the clinic was filled with a cacophony of dueling marching brass bands, fireworks, and honking. All the bands seem to play the same tunes equally loudly, but not at the same time. At first I would run to the window to see them pass, but now I would welcome the relative quiet of ordinary Nagpur traffic.

The only thing I'm finding a bit odd is that I am not at all interested in food, though I've always had a robust appetite. The food here is an important part of the treatment. It is carefully prepared. Everything is very fresh, if a little bland. But at the moment I have no interest in it. It's like something is blocking my hunger receptors. I can think of many times in recent years when I would have begged for such an eventuality, but now I think it's time for some gustatory enthusiasm. Probably tomorrow.

All my love,
Catherine

16 February 2005
Nagpur, India

Dear Ones,

My eyes are burning. My arms are covered with a rash. I am mildly depressed. My appetite is off. My feet are swollen. My back hurts. My stomach is—well—unhappy. My energy level is low. My POE, which had been processing nicely, thank you, has suddenly gone on strike. My body aches. Dr. Joshi is so pleased he's giddy. Apparently, everything is going extraordinarily well. Easy for him to say!

So apparently, I'm ready for the next step. Contrary to logic, my body is behaving splendidly. It is starting to throw off toxins like a cat shakes water off its paw. One more day of eating three teaspoons of ghee (clarified butter) twice a day, and I will be ready for the varsity POE, which will happen throughout the night tomorrow night. You can all imagine how much I'm looking forward to it.

But Dr. Joshi is very pleased by the progress so far. He has gone into his laboratory (pronounced the way Igor would: la BOUR uh tree) and come up with a unique and powerful compendium of herbs. When they arrive, he will offer a *puja* to bless them. Some of the herbs, he says, are to continue the purging, while others are designed to start nourishing and building my body, especially my muscles. The next couple of weeks will be intense. But everyone in the clinic has made it abundantly clear, in many, many ways, that they are here for no other reason than to support my healing. As the reality of their intention dawns on me, I am deeply humbled. It's one thing to have that purpose for myself, but to have others share it is more than I could ever have imagined or hoped.

In fact this entire process, beginning with the staggering generosity of so many friends, has been profoundly humbling. I am face to face with my own worst sense of myself and my ability to deem myself worthy of such love and support. Like many of us, I have no trouble imagining this worthiness in others. But for myself? It stretches credulity. And yet, here it is. I would wish some version of this experience for every one of you. It is indeed life-altering.

When I knew I was coming to India, I was faced with a dilemma. Last October, I learned the hard way that I could no longer walk without assistance. A sudden, very hard encounter with a sidewalk in Boston's South End taught me that I must, from then on, rely on a cane and a leg brace. When I trip now, which I do more and more often, I can no longer catch myself. So I became religious about using the cane and brace. Then in January, a second leg brace was added to my regalia. The beauty of the braces is that they hold my legs up when my muscles become tired, which they do quite quickly. The only problem with the braces is that they are held in place by my shoes. India is a country in which wearing shoes into someone's home or a temple or even this clinic is considered rude. Also, for all their merits, the braces are very, very hot. What to do?

I presented this dilemma to the wonderful people at Hangar Orthopedics who make my braces, and to my physiatrist, Lisa Krivickas, and my physical therapist, Joanne Clifford at Spaulding Hospital. Joanne is the one who came up with the solution, and Dr. Krivickas, with gracious speed, made the solution real. As a result, I came to India carrying a long, cardboard box. Inside was a brand new pair of forearm crutches that I use all day, every day now as I make my way around the clinic. It is becoming increasingly hot here (90 degrees today, please don't hate me New Englanders!), so I use them when I go out, too, so I can wear sandals instead of big heavy shoes. Dr. Joshi says his goal is for me to leave these crutches in India because I'll no longer need them. I'll raise a mug of ginger tea—the *panchakarma* beverage of choice—to that!

All my love,
Catherine

19 February 2005
Nagpur

Dear Ones,

Virechana!!!

It's pronounced vair-ay-chaana, and it's the varsity POE I was talking about. God may have created the world in seven days, but *ayurveda* needs eight. The eighth day is the rest day, and with good reason.

Valerie, my treatment-mate, calls this the Drano Protocol, with good reason. On the evening of the seventh day of treatment, one is presented with an innocent small plastic bag containing 10 or 11 large, soft, brown, hand-made pills. It is significant that while Mukul Joshi dispenses all the other herbs, only Dr. Joshi dispenses these little babies. They look almost cute. But knowing what they are capable of, once ingested, made me feel a bit like Socrates with the hemlock.

I was genuinely nervous as the clock approached 9:00 pm, two hours after dinner. When Dr. Joshi gave me the pills, I told him that I was concerned that virechana might unduly tax my system, which is not entirely robust. Dr. Joshi explained that he had designed a relatively mild virechana for that reason.

So I took my pills, like the warrior woman I am, and went to bed. Two hours later, awakened by an unmistakable and undeniable urge, I said "Show time!" out loud into the dark room and launched myself out of bed. Seven hours and two quarts of bodily fluids later, I was done. The after affects left me spacey, but none the worse for wear and fully appreciating why the eighth day is for rest.

I spent the day gratefully reading, doing the Globe crossword puzzle that my beloved husband had sent, and generally lazing around. Toward the end of the day, feeling pretty good, Frank and I took an auto-rickshaw down the street to buy fruit and flowers. Then Valerie, Frank, and an Indian woman named Sadhana and I had dinner, and we all went to bed. The end, I thought, to a textbook *virechana.*

But there was a wrinkle. In the middle of the night, my body decided to revisit the experience of the previous night, but much more aggressively. By morning I was decidedly unwell. What followed was a strong dose of tender loving care. My regular daily regimen was suspended. Dr. Joshi, who was at a weekend conference, was called. Mukul arrived with immediate remedies. Dr. Joshi's wife, Shalmali, who is also a doctor, arrived and took my vital signs.

As the day progressed, a very gentle but conscientious alchemy was practiced on my body. I was given some herbs, and my response to them was tracked. Depending on how my body responded, other herbs were introduced. I cannot remember when I have ever been so lovingly taken care of. Though I woke at dawn feeling wretched and worried, those feelings were dispelled quickly and firmly.

I spent the day reading and sleeping. Slowly, the symptoms subsided. Every 15 minutes or so someone would crack my door and check on me. By dinner, I was back on my feet and treated to *kichari*, a bland rice dish, and *keer*, a sort of tapioca pudding. I have been advised on healing herbs to take during the night. I doubt I'll need them. I actually feel quite wonderful.

Sadhana and I are in rooms next to each other, so we see each other constantly and have had wonderful conversations. She speaks flawless English and, thankfully, also speaks Marathi, which is what the staff here at the clinic speaks. This morning when she heard I had had a difficult night, she came immediately into my room. After scolding me for not waking her, she said "Catherineji, I will give you a healing." Immediately, everyone else left the room. After she had asked for grace, she took my head in her hands and held me for a few minutes. Immediately, I started to feel better. After she was finished, she told me that on the night she first met me, she had offered me her prayers and blessings and had been doing so every day since then. But yesterday, she said she had spoken to her guru on my behalf and she expected a response from him in a day or two. She felt certain that when I leave India, I will no longer need help in walking. The reason for this, she said, is because I am like her and the world needs our *seva*. I'll admit that for most of the morning, I felt a little weepy.

It's wonderful and instructive to be in a country where having a guru is an expected way of life. To illustrate: Two women who were patients when I first got here, found, through a rather convoluted connection, a tailor on the other side of town. They were going to see this tailor and asked if I'd like to come along. Delighted by the prospect of seeing another part of Nagpur, I said yes. At the end of a

20-minute auto-rickshaw ride, we came to a large building. Walking through the dim open-air first floor, we came to a bank of elevators, one of which worked. The tailor was located on the second floor. We entered, and while she greeted everyone, my eye caught her *puja*, or altar. (A *puja* can also mean a blessing.) There in the corner of her shop was a typical altar to a guru, and the guru was none other than Gurumayi, the same as mine! It's important to know that among Indians, Gurumayi is not especially well known. But here was an Indian devotee who has been practicing Siddha Yoga as long as I have. Her name is Ritu Sahu, and I believe I understood her to say she has been to South Fallsburg, New York. I look forward to seeing her again in a couple of days. She gave us all cards with the New Year's message in Hindi. And just when I was feeling a little far from home!

Now it is 9 pm. Mukul and Privin both just stopped by to check on me before heading home. Privin is going to the hospital to spend the night with his three-year old son who is recovering from bronchitis. I thanked them for all their care today and they thanked me in return.

Toto, we're definitely not in Kansas anymore!

All my love,
Catherine

23 February 2005
Nagpur, India

Dear Ones,

Some friends here at the clinic are about to leave, so we decided
to go to the great Ganesh Temple here and offer a puja, a blessing
for their safe travels and continued healing. We planned to go on a
weekday afternoon when the crowds would be small and the *pandits*
(holy men) would not be too busy to do a special puja just for us.
The gateman found us an auto-rickshaw driver who would take us
to the temple and wait for us. We anticipated that we would be in
the temple for about an hour. We left the clinic at around 1pm,
planning to be back for afternoon treatments by 4 o'clock. Plenty
of time!

But this is India, the land where daily rolling black outs are routine,
so here's what actually happened. We arrived at the temple to find
one pandit and many worshippers. From a vendor at the gate we
bought gift offerings of garlands, loose flowers, coconuts, incense,
and sugar pellets. The pandit took it all except the loose flowers,
which we tossed onto the altar. He adorned each of us with a big

orange *bindi*, a mark between our eyebrows. We circled the altar three times, and then sat quietly off to the side to see what would happen next. It was a hot day so it felt good to be sitting in the cool marble interior of the temple.

The temple itself is not very big. It is a large room, open on three sides, built long ago to shelter a huge tree. At the base of the tree is a very large root or bole in the shape of an elephant's head, representing Ganesh, the much-loved elephant-headed god. The image of an elephant had been painted in orange and red to emphasize the natural proportions of the root. Around the image is an enclosed area where the pandit presides. People were bowing to the image and ringing a bell to send prayers to heaven. Some worshippers were circling the image three times clockwise, and offering incense and *prasad*. Prasad is food that people bring from home or, as in our case, buy at the temple. The prasad is blessed, and then offered to others. After the coconut was blessed, Valerie took it to the pandit outside to break. She then offered it to others.

Everywhere we go, we stand out. Imagine that! As we ride along the street in an auto rickshaw, Indians poke their heads in and ask where we're from. Young people follow us through the market. So it was no surprise when, as I sat watching the activity at the temple, a young girl came and sat next to me, snuggling close. I would guess she was about 10 years old. In very good English, she asked my name and where I was from and introduced herself. Very shortly, her brother appeared at my side, and he, too, engaged me in conversation.

We had been hoping to purchase some bead *malas*, or necklaces, to have blessed for ourselves and close friends and family, so I asked the boy where we might locate some. Immediately, he put up a wait-a-minute finger and ran off. A minute later, the pandit, having left his station next to the altar, beckoned to me through an open doorway.

The pandit took us to a man outside the temple who seemed to be holding court, busily signing papers. Chairs were brought and a small crowd gathered. We watched the man conduct his business for a while longer. When he was finished, he turned to us and, in heavily accented English, compromised only by an almost complete lack of teeth, exchanged greetings. From the young man, he learned that we were looking for a particular kind of mala. He asked us to wait about 15 minutes. Then he spoke to a young man next to him, who took off at a fast trot. Next the man wanted to know if we drank tea. "Chai?" I asked. As I said their word for "tea," an appreciative murmur ran through the crowd. Of course, chai is not on the ayurvedic menu, but we instantly decided an exception could be made.

We learned that the man was the temple administrator. He told us about the temple's history and asked us about our individual relationships with God. At one point, a phone was brought to him. It was the proprietor of the shop to which he had sent the young man. He assured the shop owner that he had real Americans with cash on the line. Shortly after he hung up, the young man returned with several bags of malas. The administrator vouched for the shop owner and assured us the malas were good quality and a fair price. They were beautiful indeed, and we bought several. The transaction complete, the crowd thinned out, and we finished our chai. We thanked our benefactor and looked up to see our harried rickshaw driver standing beside us. His one-hour wait had become two. Apologizing, we hurried away. Ganesh, in his special and wonderful way, had cleared the way for grace to happen.

My daily routine has changed very little. After I recovered from virechana, I felt great. The only change in my schedule is that now I have a hatha yoga session every morning with Dr. Gauri. It's one-on-one and between the strengthening and stretching I do with her and the heat and massaging I do with Privin, my legs feel stronger and more limber than they have in months. When I first arrived in India, my legs were very weak, probably as a result of the travel. I really needed the support of the forearm crutches. Now I have regained my pre-travel strength and my legs feel like they have increased stamina. If my legs could stabilize at this stage, I would feel well-served by this experience.

However, I have discovered the downside to being pampered by the clinic staff. My left hand, the one that at home gets used for so many daily tasks, has had little to do here, and has atrophied more. So as of yesterday morning, despite kind and well-meaning protests, I now do my own dishes. It's a tough life!

Sometimes I think I would like to stay here for the rest of my life, while at other times five weeks seem very long. Tomorrow I will have been here two weeks. Amazing! The time has flown. In two days, I will be heading into my next virechana. As Galen said to me on the phone this morning, when I was remarking on apparent lack of progress, "Mom, you've only been there two weeks." So true. But what a two weeks!

All my love,
Catherine

25 February 2005
Nagpur, India

Dear Ones,

I met with Dr. Joshi this morning to let him know how I am doing and to ask more questions. He wanted to check my physical signs, give me a two-week status report, and modify the extensive list of herbs I am taking. It was an illuminating conversation.

I am heading into my second *virechana*, probably Sunday night. As happened the last time, the days leading up to the big day are almost as arduous as the event itself: migraine, aching legs, a feeling of extreme heat in my upper belly, the return of The Rash. Strangely, with the exception of The Rash, these are all symptoms I often experienced before coming to India; they are only just now appearing for the first time here. But, Dr. Joshi is very excited. He says I continue to do better than he had hoped. All of the benchmarks by which progress is measured in ayurvedic medicine are positive—well, actually, negative—because the goal is for most of these indicators to fall, not rise.

Dr Joshi told me this morning he had been reading an article in a scientific journal about current discoveries involving the particular nervous system that governs the digestive track (or the gut, as he so adamantly calls it) and the connection between disturbances in that nervous system and neurological disorders like MS, Parkinsons, and ALS. For Dr. Joshi, the timing of my visit to Nagpur is auspicious. I give him an opportunity to see firsthand how his theory and years of practice can positively affect my condition. We both benefit.

Before my meeting with Dr. Joshi this morning, I found myself contemplating the big M: Miracles. Certainly, if my work with Dr. Joshi yields not just a curtailment but a relief of symptoms, many would consider that miraculous. In fact, allopathic medicine would consider remission an unexplainable phenomenon, if not a miracle.

All along, I have been saying that my reason for coming to India was primarily for spiritual fulfillment. If any form of physical healing happened also, that would be an added boon. Since I believed I had to choose, I chose spiritual liberation. Today I found myself wondering if I haven't been a bit short-sighted.

Miracles only happened to other people, surely not to me. But what would change my perspective on the world more effectively than a good old-fashioned miracle? Once again, I need to watch out what I have been asking for. Spiritual realization had seemed much less presumptuous than asking for a miracle. But did I think realization would be some neat little moment when I would suddenly turn around and all would be clear? Baba Muktananda used to tell seekers that the only difference between a realized person and one who is not is "a slight shift in perspective." But something needs to urge that shift. Why not a miracle? Why not me?

Some lines of thinking have their own engine. Once the throttle has been let out, the vehicle wants to roll forward. So, we'll see where this goes. I figure if I can learn to say "World Champion" and "Boston Red Sox" in the same sentence, I can surely learn to say "Catherine" and "miracle" simultaneously.

Sadhana, my Indian woman friend staying here in the clinic, lent me a book today. I opened to a page that contained a single quotation: "A miracle gives a whole new meaning to life." And how would I define a miracle? Well, for me right now, I would agree with Dr. Joshi. He believes that the treatments I am responding to now can send my illness into remission, but that to see a relief of symptoms would take divine intervention. This morning, he looked across the table at me, held out his hand, and said "I'm committed to seeing how far we can go on all levels. I hope you are with me." I shook his hand. I am.

All my love,
Catherine

2 March 2005
Nagpur, India

Dear Ones,

A second virechana, and I have turned the corner. The second was as captivating as the first. Twelve hours of cheering my body on as it routed toxins out of their beds and sent them packing. POE par excellence. Then another two days to recover, watched over with great care by Dr. Joshi and his crack team of TLC experts. Today, I feel like a human being once again.

Dr. Joshi now says we have done as much cleansing as my body can handle. In fact, we've done more than he anticipated we would. It seems that as soon as my body was given the message it should divest itself of poisons, it unloaded them with an enthusiasm equal only to someone unloading stock in 1929. As in 1929, what followed was a bit of a depression. Fortunately, mine was short-lived. And now it's time to rebuild my squeaky clean system.

The next phase of treatment is specifically designed to build muscle mass. There will be more cleansings along the way—at least one more—but the emphasis now will be on restoration. Going into this, we all knew I could do cleansing. We just didn't know how, as Garrison Keillor would say, *efficacious* I would be.

I've just finished reading a book I found in the clinic library, Edward P. Jones's *The Known World*. It's a beautiful book, great storytelling, wonderful imagery, difficult subject. I realized as I read it that since arriving in Nagpur, I have been creating a similar world for myself, expanding my definition of the known world. Every day I explore my own inner and outer worlds, and every day the parameters of those worlds expand.

On my first morning here, I took a brief walk just outside the clinic gates. Today, alone, I negotiated an auto-rickshaw ride to another part of Nagpur, some 15 minutes from those same gates. As my internal world becomes stiller, I have fuller conversations with myself and can revel in my own courage and new-found freedom, freedom, as it turns out, that I always had but had rarely exercised.

One delightful aspect of Nagpur has been my discovery of the Siddha Yoga community here. In an earlier letter I mentioned an Indian clothing designer-tailor whom I met when I first arrived. Ritu is a devotee of my guru, Gurumayi. Several others at the clinic were having clothes made by Ritu, and I had gone with them to Ritu's shop a few times. Ritu put me in touch with Subhir Buty, who offered to take me to a house that was hosting the monthly community *satsang*, a program of chanting and scripture readings. I never could have found the place on my own. Directions in Nagpur are given by landmarks, not street addresses. Mapquest would be a joke here.

It turned out that the house wasn't far away. It was quite large, and programs were in a huge room on the second floor (what they call the first floor, as distinct from the ground floor here). The room was long, with large open windows at each end and an impressive array of fans circling overhead. In front of one bank of windows was the altar, with a huge picture of Gurumayi, festooned and garlanded with orange chrysanthemums. About 100 people of all ages attended. The program was run primarily by the young people and spoken entirely in Hindi. But Siddha Yoga programming is the same everywhere, so I was never really lost. At the end of the program, all of the older people introduced themselves, and offered any support or resources I might need. I have a piece of paper covered with names and phone numbers and information about upcoming programs. I think the next time we will come together is for Shivaratri, the night of the new moon that is sacred to Lord Shiva. Imagine! Shivaratri with Siddha Yoga devotees in Nagpur! Too cool!

In anticipation of Scott's arrival, I have moved to a larger room. It's at the top corner of the building in the back and is just beautiful. My treatment schedule for Saturday has been rearranged so I can accompany Mukul to the airport to pick up Scott. Having him here will be an opportunity to bring someone else into the embrace of my known world.

All my love,
Catherine

6 March 2005
Nagpur, India

Dear Ones,

During my first week here, I read Elizabeth Bowen's *The House in Paris*. At one point, one of the characters is reveling in a period of delicious solitude. She is acutely aware of her delight in being alone and comments that it's so wonderful she'd like to share it. The comment truly spoke to my own feelings. I have loved my time here in Nagpur: the solitude, the ability to set my own pace and agenda, to delight in my own perception of this world and all it has given me. I have loved it so much that I have been wanting more and more to share it. And just when that desire was most intense, I went to the airport with Mukul on Saturday morning and watched my very weary husband get off the plane from Mumbai.

So Scott is here now, at just the right moment. Dr. Joshi welcomed him with open arms and began his *panchakarma* immediately. By the end of today, Scott was completely embraced by this new world and has gotten to know some of the other patients. Today was Sunday, a half day here at the clinic, so tomorrow he will have an opportunity to get to know the staff when things begin for him in earnest. In the meantime, today I took him on a walk down the street for his first taste of Nagpur. I am delighted that he has come to join me.

And the timing is perfect. As I turn the corner and begin the more experimental phase of my treatment, his company will make an enormous difference. I was becoming a little lonely, and his being here allows me to relax a bit more. I am noticing in this new phase that I am feeling physically stronger and more limber. I now have an hour of customized hatha yoga everyday, and the improvement in my mobility is notable. Perhaps it is the warm, dry climate. Perhaps it is the twice-daily full-body massages. Perhaps it is the physical discipline of the yoga, coupled with an environment dedicated to relaxation and calm. Perhaps it is the herbs and the *panchakarma* regimen. Probably it's the totality of all of that. The next two weeks will be very instructive.

While the internal, physical adventure advances, the external adventure of being in India also continues. Last week I was invited to Ritu Sahu's home. Ritu is a Siddha Yogi whom I met by happy coincidence during my first week here, and we have seen each other a few more times for *chai* and conversation at her shop. As a single woman, Ritu still lives at home with her parents, and she was very keen that I meet them, especially her father. She explained that her father is a spiritual healer and a follower of the healer Sai Baba.

Ritu explained to me that Sai Baba's healing energy works through her father, whom she knew would want to meet me. So last Thursday night, guru's day, her cousin picked me up at the clinic. As it happens, that afternoon I had gotten a migraine. Privin tried to work on it, but by evening the migraine was in full bloom. However, no little headache was going to get in the way of this meeting.

At the apartment, Ritu's mother and aunt offered me *namaste* and seated me on a cushy red chair. Then her father came in and greeted me in excellent English. He is a small dark man, with piercing brown eyes. His eyes reminded me of my father's, but without a hint of the fear that always haunted my father's eyes. Her father sat in the chair next to mine, and focused on me as if I were the only person in the room. The older women remained silent. Ritu spoke occasionally, but mostly deferred to her father.

Without any preamble, he began explaining his cosmology. It was the same as my spiritual worldview. When I said "And I am God," he said "And so we understand each other." Even his understanding of my illness is the same as mine, that somehow my spiritual, physical, and cosmic bodies are out of alignment. He talked a little about why he thought I had gotten this particular malady and his firm belief that I would be completely cured of it. He also told me that the key to my good health was in the full realization that I am God and that everything comes from God. Once I know this, beyond a shadow of a doubt, I will know that all healing comes from God and that God can do anything. He emphasized that this healing required the alignment of the three bodies.

He continued talking, but my head was in so much pain that I told him we had to stop. Immediately, he jumped up, went across the room to his desk, put something on his fingertips, and came back. He had me remove my glasses and then started touching my head, sometimes firmly and sometimes softly. Finally, he pressed a *bindi* into my forehead. My head still hurt, but I felt very calm. He retreated to the opposite side of the room and just watched me for a few minutes. Shortly, Ritu brought me a glass of water.

Then she invited us to come in to dinner. She knew my dietary restrictions—God bless her for even considering them!—and had made a wonderful meal, but just at that moment, my migraine went into my stomach and I couldn't eat anything. I apologized and her father said, "Don't apologize. This home is your home now. I knew you would be coming, and now you are here. You must feel completely comfortable and not worry about anything." I told them I needed to go back to the clinic. Immediately, the cousin was called and everyone got up to say goodbye.

I shook hands with Ritu's mother and aunt, but when I went to say goodbye to her father, he took both my hands and I was suddenly overwhelmed with love for him. I embraced him, kissed him on the cheek, and out of my mouth came: "Papa." No one was more surprised than I was. The women laughed and so did he. He said "Yes, you are now like a daughter to me." I was deeply moved. Then Ritu walked me down to the car and thanked me—*she* thanked *me!*—for coming.

The next day, as Privin was giving me my morning massage, an image popped into my mind—one of those huge bank vault combination locks, like the ones in old bank caper movies. In order for the vault to open and reveal its treasures, all of the tumblers have to line up. Because this is a big, magnificent vault, the lock is made of precious metals and moves smoothly and soundlessly, making only the slightest click when the tumblers align. I am that lock. My various bodies are the tumblers. They are now moving, slowly, smoothly, silently. I'm just waiting for the sound of those clicks.

All my love,
Catherine

17 March, 2005
Nagpur

Dear Ones,

As my time here in India draws to a close, I ask myself once again, why am I here? What is this time for? The catch-all response is "healing." But healing what? The most obvious answer is: my body. But in India everything seems to point directly toward or away from one's relationship with God. So why did I come here for this healing?

This trip affords a rare opportunity. I am here to contemplate my death and ultimately, I hope, to embrace it with joy. How many of us are given five weeks to devote to an almost full-time focus on the inevitable? Looking back now, I am impatient; (I'm often impatient, Dr. Joshi points out). Have I squandered this time? At the moment, I don't feel I've made any significant progress, physically, emotionally, or spiritually. But at least I've distilled the question, and know that even after I leave here, transformations will continue.

If we have faith in grace, from whatever source, we know that our own efforts play an important role in attracting grace. On the subject of our ultimate demise, what form can and should our efforts take?

If death is inevitable, what effort is required? If our desire is, indeed, NOT to die, should that be the focus of our effort, no matter how futile ? And what form might grace take? Grace cannot, and I think is not meant to, spare us from death. So this dance between grace and self-effort is temporal. It is a dance only for today, in fact, a dance for this moment in time.

What do I want? In simple terms, I want a good life and a good death. I have the former. That is what makes the prospect of leaving so painful. I sometimes ask, only half joking, why God couldn't have given me a miserable life, one I would gladly leave? But no, the good life of my intention, I have. So what about the good death? What exactly is a good death, for me, if not for others? I am resolved that a good death would include blissful awareness of the truth.

In every way, this is what my time in India has been about. Am I resolved and blissfully aware now? No, not yet. But everything about my time with Dr. Joshi has been designed to move me to this new perspective and keep me moving once I return home. How could I ask for a greater gift than this?

As I have mentioned, one goal of this trip was to celebrate Shivaratri here in India with Scott. Shivaratri is a Hindu rite celebrated on the first day of the new moon in late February or early March. The new moon specifically honors God in the form of Shiva. It's a day for experiencing, acknowledging, and celebrating the power of the divine. According to custom, singing God's name on Shivaratri is like opening a channel from your lips to God's ears. Hindus chant Shiva chants.

Originally, Scott and I thought we would attend the local Siddha Yoga community's Shivaratri festivities. But by now we had learned the need to remain flexible here. A few days before, we learned that the local program would conflict with our treatment times at the clinic. I had to remind myself, very sternly, of why I am here, and chose to forego the program.

However, there is a terrace on the roof of the clinic. It has a lovely, enclosed area with a deep green travertine floor. At sunrise and sunset every day, David, a patient from Oregon, goes up there and offers a *yagna*, or sacred fire. So David, Scott and I decided that if we couldn't go to Shivaratri, we would bring Shivaratri to us.

In the afternoon between treatments, David went shopping for plenty of ghee (clarified butter) to keep a strong fire going. Scott and I obtained some cut flowers, a flowered garland, candles, and a white cloth to cover the chair that would serve as our altar. At sunset, David would offer his yagna and the attendant mantras. And we would all follow that with an hour of chanting *Om Namah Shivaya* a traditional mantra that means Honor the God within you. We invited the entire clinic, both patients and staff, to join us.

We all assembled on the roof terrace. Just as David began to chant, an enormous wind blew up. Flames danced and the trees swayed wildly around us in the accumulating darkness. As David chanted, the wind intensified. When we switched to chant the *Om Namah Shivaya*, rain began to pound on the corrugated roof of the terrace and to spray in through the open sides of the pavilion. We chanted on, and at the end of the chant, silence descended. The storm came to an abrupt stop. We sat in the silence for a few minutes and then went in. Later in the night the storm returned, along with hail! Nagpurians have since told us that it often rains on Shivaratri, but that this year's rains were epic. We would have to agree.

The morning after Shivaratri, I was examined by one of Dr. Joshi's colleague's, who asked about the physically demanding work I'd been doing at The Home Depot when ALS symptoms first became evident. The physical exertion and weight loss of that period (I had lost 15 pounds) seemed to represent a triggering effect for a number of the traditional Asian doctors and healers whom I've consulted. Later that evening, Dr. Joshi met with me again, and he seemed to suggest that a recent stomach flare-up was in some way connected to the ALS.

My heart skipped a beat. I passed a wakeful night frantically replaying the end of the conversation with Dr. Joshi and his apparent implication that the ALS had spread into my stomach. I cried, slept, woke, cried some more. At dawn, Scott work up and I shared the night's news with him. He cried also, but was also an enormous comfort. I am so grateful he is here!

As others began to wake up, we got dressed and joined in the normal activities of the day. One of the morning rituals is the daily panchakarma status report. We are all required to describe on a form and in lurid detail the activities of our bowels during the previous 24 hours. At the bottom is a space that allows us to send Dr. Joshi any specific messages or information we think he might need to know for the treatment day ahead. That morning, I wrote: "I spent the night crying. I am overwhelmed with feelings of hopelessness. My goal today is to reestablish my equilibrium."

But equilibrium was hard won. Lying on the massage table that morning, my weeping began again. Alarmed, Privin notified Dr. Joshi. Before the massage was over, I got the message that Dr. Joshi was on his way and wanted to see me immediately. Showered, dressed, and just barely dry-eyed, I was ushered into his office. As soon as I sat down, he looked across his desk at me and declared, "I never said your ALS had spread. You have completely misunderstood. Please put that thought from your mind."

I was stunned for two reasons. For the first time I had misunderstood something Dr. Joshi had said and had therefore worried for nothing. Secondly, Dr. Joshi seemed to be clairvoyant. How did he know so precisely what was troubling me? I hadn't told him. He scolded me soundly for jumping so readily to embrace bad news. He wanted to know how our work together could possibly proceed if he was working so hard and yet I gave up hope. I felt exceedingly sheepish.

I also wondered about his powers of ESP, until he brought out Scott's morning daily status report. There, at the bottom, Scott had written: "I'm feeling very sad today at the news that Catherine's illness has spread into her stomach." Ah ha! So, no ESP, just a wonderful husband doing what he does best and a magnificent, passionate, and compassionate doctor.

To my bemusement and amazement, despite Dr. Joshi's assurances, my tears kept flowing for several more hours. Later, Privin explained to me that tears that come from the heart take longer to finish.

A misunderstanding can be a blessing. I look back on Shivaratri and see an evening of titanic external turmoil followed by a day and a night of equally dramatic internal turmoil. It's easy to see the hand of God in nature's extremes. The storm was magnificent. It was as though the wind and rain swept up the sound of the mantras in their embrace and dispersed them out over the rooftops of Nagpur. But the blessings of my internal storm were more clandestine.

Now I realize that another element was at play in my misunderstanding of Dr. Joshi. Since being diagnosed with ALS, every encounter I have had with a doctor has ended with some discouraging news. A trial medication was not working, the disease had spread to another muscle group, an area already involved had worsened, etc. My family and I have come to dread these doctor visits because of the period of sadness and depression that inevitably follows. Despite the unfailingly positive nature of my experience here, I once again was subconsciously readying myself for bad news. When it seemed to come, I embraced it.

But I am in a calmer, quieter state as a result of *panchakarma*. This time when the gathering storm broke, it swept in completely. It was violent and all-consuming. There was no managing or resisting its turbulence, as I would have attempted to do at home. It had me, and I could only agree to participate fully.

I have always known that the ayurvetic treatment would be thorough. As much as it would address the physical, it would also address the emotional, in ways no less powerful. For the healing to be complete, every aspect of my being had to be involved. It took a misunderstanding to accomplish this. As Indians say so perfectly, with an upward sweep of the hand: *Swaha!* So be it!

This is the form grace is taking. This morning the clinic is reverberating with the sound of the *Gayatri Mantras*. Over and over the Sanskrit words are repeated:

> *May we know that enlightened soul among enlightened souls;*
> *May we meditate on that supreme realized soul;*
> *May that enlightened one inspire us.*

I have begun my re-entry. Most of my treatments ended yesterday. Return transportation has been arranged. I am subtly shifting into travel mode and looking forward to going home. My time here has passed in a blink. My heart feels soft at the prospect of leaving and also at the prospect of reunion. My life is perfect. As I go forward, the transformation of panchakarma will continue to unfold. It may be so subtle that I won't notice it at first; others who know me well may need to point out the changes. I have always said that when I become fully realized, my mind will be the last to know. So it will be with this.

We leave Nagpur Sunday evening, March 20th. On Tuesday morning, we will go to Ganeshpuri for the day and then come straight back to the airport for the flight home. Our last day is ambitious, but it will allow us to be in Ganeshpuri to celebrate our 30th wedding anniversary. What could be more perfect? We'll see!

All my love,
Catherine

25 March 2005
Boston, Massachusetts

Dear Ones,

Unless one writes science fiction, I think jet lag is the closest we humans come to experiencing a rupture in the space-time continuum. It's 4:30 in the morning, and I am wide awake. My body is back in Boston, but the rest of me is still elsewhere.

After over 15 years of practicing Siddha Yoga meditation, Scott and I were adamant that we should spend March 22, our 30th wedding anniversary, in Ganeshpuri, the auspicious place Siddha Yoga calls home.

Ganeshpuri was nothing but a small clearing in the jungle when the holy man Bhagawan Nityananda appeared there sometime in the 1940s or 1950s. He was originally from South India, but very little else is known about him except that he was one of the great saints of modern India. Nityananda is revered throughout the world, but nowhere more so than in Ganeshpuri. It was in Ganeshpuri that Swami Muktananda found Nityananda, recognized him as his guru, and received spiritual initiation from him. It was also in Ganeshpuri that Swami Muktananda gave initiation to Swami Chidvilasananda. Historically, a lot has happened in this tiny village. At present it contains both the mother ashram for Siddha Yoga and a magnificent temple to Bade Baba (Bhagawan Nityananda). It certainly seemed like the perfect place to spend our last day in India and our anniversary.

We had been told to expect a two or three hour car ride each way from Mumbai, so we planned to spend the day. But plans here are a malleable concept. We had no idea what to expect in Ganeshpuri, but friends had told us it was beautiful.

The ashram is officially restricted to people on retreat, but I had tried to let the ashram manager know we were coming, hoping we might be allowed to stand inside briefly. However, that was not to be. An officious and humorless man at reception let us know in no uncertain terms that "This is a retreat site, not a tourist attraction." Excuse me? He told us we could sit in the garden across the road from the ashram, and could attend the chanting of the noontime arati at a shrine at the entrance to the ashram, where there was a statue of Bade Baba. In other words, our presence would be tolerated.

So we sat in the beautiful garden where there was a lovely breeze, and then walked back across the road to the shrine. There we received a true welcome—from the security guards. They could not have been friendlier or more gracious. After singing the familiar arati, we felt restored and complete. We prepared to go into the village, where a treat awaited us.

The village of Ganeshpuri itself surrounds a main road. Where this road bisects the ashram, it is wide and serene, but in the half-mile that separates the ashram from the village, it becomes narrow and busy. Cars, ox carts, motorbikes, bicycles, auto-rickshaws, pedestrians, and all manner of animal life jockey for space. Shops and residences crowd the road on both sides. Near the Nityananda Temple, the population swells even more. The midday arati was just beginning in the Temple when we arrived. Hurriedly, we purchased the requisite offerings—garland, loose flowers, coconut, herbs, and sugar pellets to be blessed and shared.

The Temple looks like a large white drip castle and is exquisitely beautiful. The large courtyard surrounding the temple had been baking in the sun. Our soft white feet were no match for the fiery surface and removing my shoe and leg brace was tricky. We hopped and jumped across the hot flagstones, and hurried upstairs and inside.

The Temple is a large, open air room with a huge golden *murti*, or statue, of Bhagawan Nityananda in a large enclosure at one end. Brahmin priests performed rituals around the resplendent statue. There was a nice breeze and a few fans. Scott took our offering tray and joined the men on the left, while I went around to the right to sit on the floor with the women. There were several hundred people, primarily Indian, seated quietly along the walls. The lone exception was an ecstatic western woman, seated toward the center, weaving with the chant and gesticulating wildly.

Suddenly, the chanting ended and temple guards formed the men and women into formal lines along the sides of the room. For the next 45 minutes, alternating lines of women and men wound toward the front of the room for Bade Baba's blessing. Many people carried offering trays like ours. Somehow, Scott and I were the last in our lines to approach and could do so together. As Scott presented our offerings, the priest greeted him with a hearty "Hi ya!" He took our flowers and laid them lovingly at Bade Baba's feet, broke our coconut, and returned it to us. Later, we gave this blessed coconut to our driver who accepted it enthusiastically.

I stepped up for my moment of *darshan,* of being in a holy presence, and had my first opportunity to look into the face of the murti. Unlike other statues of Bade Baba that I am used to, the face of this one is deeply and finely etched and looks idiosyncratically human. I was surprised and captivated by how he seemed to consume me with his look. I brought out the packet of necklaces we had had made in Nagpur and offered them to Bade Baba for his blessing. We regarded each other for another moment, I bowed, and was then ushered out the door. "This," I thought, "is why we came to Ganeshpuri—for the simplicity and beauty of that moment."

When we got back to the car to return to Mumbai, I was suddenly overcome with fatigue. I thought "I've had enough of strangeness. I want to go home." But my feelings had little to do with the unfamiliar and everything to do with knowing that my adventure was complete.

By the time we were finally at the airport and on the plane, cued up for our 2:40 a.m. departure, we could feel our brains gently yielding to the force of gravity and starting to settle in our feet. I remember walking down the jetway and the flight attendant's "Bon soir." I remember sitting, fastening my seat belt, and pulling the blanket up to my chin. I slept, nearly bolt upright, for 6 straight hours.

Two days later, I'm still mostly sleeping. I'm discovering the immense difference a ten and a half hour time gap can make. I'm rediscovering the even greater difference between New England's chilly weather and Nagpur's. And I am struck, not for the first time, by what a significant difference a mentor can make. When I wanted to dance, I had Cheryl Cutler to guide, inspire, and nurture me. When I wanted to administer the arts, I had Jeanne Beaman. When I wanted to be a good mother, I had Jane Nagel and Ruth Roehrig.

When I wanted to be a successful businesswoman, I had Eleanor Hughes. When I wanted to be a good wife, I had Scott Nagel. Now I want to understand and experience true healing and have been given a generous community of friends and the unqualified love and support of Sunil Joshi.

I will see him again when he comes to Boston in May. He believes I should begin another panchakarma in January 2006, if not earlier. In the meantime, I have a daily ayurvedic regimen that includes everything I had at the clinic with the exception—sob!—of daily massages. And when I say everything, I mean EVERYTHING. 'Nuff said.

All my love,
Catherine

Part Two

14 May 2005

Dear Ones,

I have been home quite a while now, and India seems both immediate and a long time ago. I came home gratefully—grateful to have been blessed with the supreme adventure that was India, and grateful to be back among the familiar and beloved.

And yet, somewhere over the Atlantic on my way home, a dense fog descended over me. At first, I put it down to getting used to the 10 and a half hour time change and the 65 degree drop in temperature. But the feeling of fuzzy disconnect persisted—for weeks.

Fortunately, Dr. Joshi had warned that panchakarma doesn't end when the treatments stop. The intense transformation that the body experiences as a result of the cleansing continues for months. He told us we might find ourselves feeling unusually sensitive, both emotionally and physically. He also cautioned that we might experience periods of depression. He made a particular point of this with me. At the time, I laughed and said, "Oh, you mean, don't make any big decisions and don't operate heavy machinery."

In fact, these weeks since my return have included all that he warned us about. When the fog of re-entry began to lift, the woman I found staring back at me in the mirror was changed. For one thing, I had lost 20 pounds—not a bad thing. But this same woman was also raging with white hot anger.

Inanimate objects are not safe in my company. Suddenly, the frustrations of my disability have become untenable. I am unsteady on my feet. I trip. I drop and bump into things. I knock things over. I have trouble doing simple things for myself. I am perpetually having to ask for help. I have to move slowly and cautiously. Someone watching me navigate might reasonably assume I am drunk. These are not new things, but suddenly they are unbearable. When I am not angry, I am depressed. It's been one hell of a homecoming.

Underlying all this has been my desire to find an answer to the question so many of you have asked me since I returned. It's the obvious question, the one I knew would come and yet have felt inadequate to answer clearly. Did the trip help—was it worth it?

The quick answer is that there was no fast-acting miracle. The physical symptoms of ALS continue to progress. I have come home neither cured nor in remission. But that's an inadequate and incomplete answer. As my lovely goddaughter asked when I gave her this answer, "Yes, Catherine, but what about the journey?"

And contemplating the journey does, indeed, tell a fuller story. The trip to India was worth every moment. It's something I had always wanted to do, so a life's quest has been satisfied. I got there and back successfully and had experiences filled with wonder and delight. So, while I may not be feeling physically powerful, I still live a very full life. A diagnosis like ALS can naturally generate hopelessness. I choose to see it otherwise. In the presence of reasonable possibilities, I chose to take a chance. I chose to honor the possibility and the adventure. Why not?

Dr. Joshi has told me that I should not look for noticeable results of the panchakarma until July or August. Of course, I am impatient. I want results now. Patience may be a virtue, but it isn't one of mine. He sent me home with an entire suitcase full of herbs, oils, and syrups. I have these, my diet, my regimen of meditation, massage, and yoga. I am being amazingly faithful to all of them. I will continue to honor the possibility and the adventure. As I said before, "Why not?"

I will see Dr. Joshi here in Boston next week. The saga continues.

All my love,
Catherine

18 May 2005

Dear Ones,

If that last update seemed a bit lugubrious, it's all part of this game I call "Living While Dying." To be honest, it's a game we're all playing. I'm just, perhaps, a little more aware of moving the joystick than others. For me, some days (weeks!) are cheerier than others. And there's nothing that adds cheer to a week like a delightful distraction. This past week afforded a beauty—beautiful in every sense of the word. It was Scott's exhibit of photographs (or as he calls them, photomicrographs) at the Boston Society of Architects (www.architects.org).

Scott is a geologist, but he is more than that. For many years, one of the consulting services Scott has offered is something called petrographic analysis. Its purpose is to help his clients know the composition of the rock on which they propose to build a building or through which they want to bore a tunnel. In a process a bit like an earth biopsy, a sample of the rock is taken and sent to Scott who arranges for it to be shaved so thin as to be transparent. This slim shaving, called—with typical engineering dispatch—a thin section, is then epoxied onto a glass microscope slide.

Remember biology class? Not the dissecting part, not the counting fruit flies part, but the looking through the microscope at the cells of green leaves part? Remember those neatly ordered rows of green cells marching across the lens? That's what Scott sees when he looks at the thin rock sections under the microscope—only ecstatically *disarrayed*. Instead of monochromatic, tidy rows, he sees explosions of color and shape and form. Rocks are studies in gray and brown, right? Not so. Under the microscope, their true colors shine through, as if in a kaleidoscope, though without a kaleidoscope's symmetry.

For years, it was a simple matter for me to know when Scott was working on a petrographic analysis. My day would be punctuated by the sound of his voice exclaiming: "Oh, wow! Come see this one!" Technicolor snowflakes—no two alike.

Subscribing to the adage "A picture's worth a thousand words," Scott devised a way to photograph the images he saw through the microscope (hence, photomicrograph) as a way to illustrate his analysis. Many of the photographs were stunningly beautiful. "Hmmm . . . ," we pondered, "If we think they're beautiful, we shouldn't keep them to ourselves. Maybe others would enjoy them, too." And so was born a series of postcards, highlighting Scott's favorite image of the moment. He sent them to his client list—a tough audience—and, of course, to our family. The latter group, naturally, deemed them brilliant. However, if a group of engineers, geologists, and construction managers were charmed, *that* would be something.

The postcards were a hit. Scott would go into clients' offices and find the postcards mounted on the wall. Some announced with pride that they were collecting the full set. As a business development tool, they were stellar. However, more than one client (and a growing list of family and friends) began to wonder aloud: "What would they look like if they were bigger—much bigger?" Scott is a geologist, a discipline between science and art. The scientist in him wanted to know the technical answer to the question. The artist wanted to investigate the possible.

And so began a three-year saga, a journey that introduced him to new photographic and computer technology, and a new professional circle of color print specialists, framers, and gallery owners. In the end, the journey led back to himself and his willingness to see an idea through to its fruition.

Today I am sitting in the midst of that fruition. The show opened at the Boston Society of Architects last week. Many of you came to celebrate the milestone with us. And now, three days a week, until the show closes on June 10th, I gallery-sit.

The gallery boasts great views. On two walls are Scott's photographs. On two walls are large windows looking out onto Broad Street, a very busy scene. Both views remind me that I am part of a larger and infinitely mysterious landscape. In the largeness of the street scene, I see the bustle of people going about the details of their daily lives. On the walls I see evidence of one of God's little secrets. You pick up a rock. Maybe you like its shape or design. There is little hint of the magnificence that lies within. The title of the exhibit is "The Stone You Kick Aside." Our in-house working title is "What God Sees."

When I look at the images in this show, I am persistently reminded of how little I know. And on the days when I feel burdened by the knowledge of what my future may hold, I look at these photos and remember that, in fact, I really don't know anything.

All my love,
Catherine

31 May 2005

Dear Ones,

In Nagpur, my known world was sensory experience. It was defined by what I saw, felt, smelled, heard, and tasted. It was all new, and the newness allowed me sublime access to wonder. The very foreignness of it sustained my delight. All my senses were wide open, all the time. And, although things often felt unfamiliar, I never felt lost.

One afternoon in Nagpur, I had a date to have tea with Ritu, the dressmaker, at her shop. By then I was quite good at hailing an auto rickshaw, negotiating the price, and sailing off into the midday heat. In fact, there were even a couple of drivers I was getting to know. I felt pretty confident and knew the route we would take across town.

First we would travel up the wide boulevard of High Court Road, past government buildings and residential compounds. Then we would turn right into a more populated area. Soon would come a traffic circle, and after taking a right, we would pass the large dog sleeping in the road. The first time I saw this dog, I thought he might be dead. But no, each time I passed, he was sleeping in a new position. After the dog, and a curving left turn, we would emerge onto a busy thoroughfare, often punctuated by small clusters of cattle. Soon, the abundant fruit market would appear on our left, and, at the next intersection, we would arrive at Ritu's building.

But on this day there was a new driver. Rather than take the usual route, the driver went straight on into an area of the city I had never seen. Shortly, he took a left into a one-lane alley that ran through a tightly settled neighborhood. For a moment, I was concerned. The likelihood of my having contracted with a rogue driver crossed my mind. But all my senses assured me that I was safe, and somehow I settled back in my seat and took in a part of India few tourists ever see. Sure enough, within a few moments we emerged from a little street out onto the busy city thoroughfare that I recognized, complete with cattle.

While I was mapping my physical world in India, I was also becoming acquainted with an internal world that valued sense over reason. Much like Nagpur itself, this internal world was new to me. I welcomed it with the same openness. When I came home, however, a strange phenomenon occurred. I returned to my familiar, previously mapped world, and my bold awareness retreated. Taking life for granted again, for almost two months I failed to notice, on any conscious level, my own remapping. At the age of 56, my internal known world has been expanding. This new exploration makes my momentary uncertainty in the back of the auto rickshaw look like a mild case of indigestion.

My short stay in Nagpur created a powerful metaphor for my life going forward. I look back on those six brief weeks, and see the groundwork for everything that has followed. Now, of course, I am my own driver. But I am like someone who has taken a professional driving course. I drive differently now, and am acutely aware of the difference. I am more confident and more daring, more inclined to go places I have not been before, despite warnings that danger may lie ahead.

Ayurveda explains that after years of incompletely digesting food, gunk called *ama* collects in our alimentary canals. When Scott used to do biohazard work, he had a colleague who described the toxins they found with the generic term "Ethelmethyl bad-shit." Ama is the ethelmethyl bad-shit of the ayurvedic world. The buildup of ama is what causes all our trouble. Ama comes in many forms (like that stuff that exits the body during panchakarma), but it also comes in the form of intense emotion.

Looking back over the last six months, I see a pattern. The treatments in India, and prior to going to India, emphasized the physically rigorous. In the month following my return home, there was a period of quiet. During the past month, however, panchakarma intensity has returned with an emphasis on emotional rigor. I'm glad I didn't know about this in advance. I might have chickened out.

I have never known anger like the rage I am experiencing now. The other day I pummeled a poor, defenseless wall phone. I could not reach someone I was trying to call. Thank God phones are made of sturdy stuff. And when hammering the phone proved unrewarding, I found a few doors to slam. In retrospect, it sounds almost funny, but this unaccustomed, overwhelming, ferocious anger destroyed my equilibrium. Afterwards, I sat alone, devastated, wondering who this person could possibly be and feeling a sensation akin to poison coursing through my body. I'm not used to expressing anger. It feels like a perilous business. I don't like it.

Here's what I'm learning: Anger is confusing and complex. I'm told expressing anger is healthy, but how does one do it without hurting or frightening the people you love? Anger is intense. It's a car that drives itself. I've got my hands on the wheel and my feet on the pedals, but its speed and trajectory are well beyond my control. How does one survive this? Anger is humiliating. I think of myself as a higher order being. I am reasonable. I am compassionate. I am understanding. I don't lose my temper. I don't have to. I am, dare I say, above such base emotion. Really? So who is this mad woman, frothing at the mouth, swearing and yelling and pounding? She can't be me, but she is. How embarrassing. How frightening. How awesome.

We all have tigers. This is mine. This is what she looks like. She's mine, and at the moment, she's huge. Her mere presence has the power to shake the ground under my feet. Her roar is so deafening as to block out all other sound. Knowing she is prowling in the vicinity is enough to keep me wary and watchful, on constant guard. She may appear at any moment. Her actions have grave consequences and are wholly unpredictable. I am well out of my element. Without wanting to sound overly dramatic, I feel mortal fear.

Writing, and therefore reading, about my adventures in India was entertaining. It was exotic and fun. Even the grisly details of panchakarma had a certain jaunty appeal. I loved the comic potential of it all. Even as my body was in extremis, I could maintain a mostly arm's-length relationship with my experience. Now the experience continues, but the location has changed. The enchanted landscape is no longer out there; it's in here. Everything important that happened to me in India lives inside me now, and I carry it with me.

My story may be far less entertaining now, but for me it is more compelling. Keeping my experience at arm's-length in order to tell a good story has become much more difficult, as you may have noticed.

There are times when my writing sounds positively whiny, even to me. My sense of humor seems to be in abeyance.

Have you noticed how often I ask you to bear with me? Well, I'm going to say it again. I went to Nagpur for healing; healing could take any number of forms. I could be cured of ALS. Or the progression of my symptoms could slow down or could stop altogether. Or I could simply come to accept with serenity and grace the outcome that God has planned for me. Now wouldn't that be something?

The process of healing is on the march. There's no doubt of that. Somehow I will pass through this phase. My tiger will become my ally, not my enemy. I can say these things, but I also have to do them. If you can, bear with me still.

All my love,
Catherine

17 June 2005

Dear Ones,

For two weeks now my tiger has been on the prowl. I am aware of her lurking. From time to time, she makes a sudden move in my direction and then, just as suddenly, withdraws. I feel I'm being stalked and toyed with. But she is in no hurry.

For a while I was super vigilant, looking for her at every opportunity. But now I have grown less wary; sometimes I forget about her entirely. But then her essence rubs against me and brings back my awarenes. She's not looking for an easy kill and she isn't sneaky. She's looking to meet me face-to-face, head-on; she's waiting for the worthy battle. At least that's how it seems when I suddenly find myself angrily throwing random objects or swearing vehemently at some minor transgression.

What a lovely metaphor this is. I can hardly get enough of it. Yet at the same time this image has been playing itself out for me, another one has presented itself. In 1941, the great playwrights George S. Kaufman and Moss Hart wrote *The Man Who Came to Dinner*. The plot involves a perfectly dreadful man who arrives for dinner and won't leave. He offends everyone delightfully. At one point, he turns to a woman hovering in a doorway and declares: "Don't ooze out. Get out." I've been feeling a lot that way myself lately. Things seem to be oozing rather than getting, and I'm finding it very irritating.

I put all of this irritation and anger down to the conflict between what I want and what is. My mind can go on and on reminding me of the way things used to be and filling me with dreadful anticipation of the way things are likely to be, banging back and forth between past and future like the clapper in a bell. The noise is deafening, and at times I would do almost anything to get it to stop. At those times, suddenly, my thoughts can become so clear they almost seem practical. If the future looks so bleak, why participate in it? Why knowingly become such a burden? Why agree to go forward? Don't ooze out, get out.

At other times I think of the irony of my diagnosis. I have had ALS for four years. Most people with typical ALS would be dead after four years. At first, I rejoiced to think that the disease in me is progressing more slowly. But now I'm not so sure. There is almost too much time to think. Don't ooze out, get out.

I want to do something definitive, get on with things, not wait like some hapless victim for the worst to descend, but somehow use the present to affect the future. But this is all in my head. My heart, when I can stop and listen to it, prescribes patience and offers comfort; it lives only in the present. And when I'm in communion with my heart, all is well. I'm just not there as often as I'd like to be. (I need to pick up the pace on the meditation practice, no doubt about it!)

In terms of doing things, Scott and I have come to the decision that we will need to move. Our home of the past almost 30 years is a large, four-story Victorian. Even before I developed ALS, we had a dawning awareness that this wonderful house no longer really suited our needs. But now, as the stairs become less and less navigable, what had previously been a gentle urge has become a necessity.

Many of you have done this thing I am dreading, many times. You have moved, and you're good at it. I used to be good at it. During the first 21 years of my life, I moved 21 times! By the time we had lived in this house—Larchmont St.—three years, I had already lived here longer than I had ever lived anywhere. We have loved this house. It has been generous and good to us. Both children were born in the upstairs corner bedroom. There have been weddings, gala birthday parties, neighborhood celebrations, short and long-term guests, and all the other gatherings and jubilations that such a large and generous house invites. But now it's clear to us that the house is ready for new energy, and we are ready for new surroundings.

At first, I found the prospect of moving devastating. But my dismay has very quickly been replaced by optimism and buoyant anticipation. Now I realize my reluctance had nothing to do with the end result and everything to do with the process of moving. There is something insidious about the nature of long term habitation. Where did all this stuff come from! Silly me, I had thought that by periodically cleaning out the occasional closet I was staying on top of the situation. What was I thinking? Now the prospect of clearing all our clutter away has immersed me in jell-o. I look at what needs to be done and feel myself moving in slow motion. Don't ooze out, get out.

So here's what we're looking for: someone wonderful to buy our house and lavish it with attention. In all of the years we've lived here, we've had a running gag. When people ask us when we will finish working on our house (because we are always working on our house), we tell them that our house will be finished when we buy that split-level in Randolph. A split level in Randolph has always been our idea of hell.

Funny how things change. Well, okay, we're not looking for a split-level. Nor are we thinking of moving to Randolph. But we are thinking along ranch house lines—one level, two-car garage, full basement. We're wondering if such confirmed city dwellers can find what looks to be very suburban living without having to leave the city. Are we asking for too much? I like to think not.

Scott's trip to Taiwan is still on hold, so until he leaves, we're working on the house. He's painting, I'm sorting. I think one of the neighbors wants the piano. I'm trying to find homes for some very large plants. Later this summer, one sister who has just been through a move herself will come and help me clear out; and the other sister, an eBay genius, will come later to make us all fabulously wealthy by selling off attic treasures.

And what of my treatments? I find it most curious that when I reported to you on my meeting with Dr. Joshi, I neglected to mention a very important item. Guess what! *Bastis* are back! Dr. Joshi was so thrilled with my progress, or lack thereof, that he assigned me a new round of these self administered treatments. Well, no wonder I'm having so much fun!

So we need boxes, painters, weeders, and the participation of anyone who understands about moving. We bought this house at auction almost 30 years ago—we've never actually bought a house in the normal way. But though we are new to this, some of you aren't. Share your wisdom please! Right now, we're going from oozing to genuine getting out.

All my love,
Catherine

27 June 2005

Dear Ones,

How often the thing we need to do is right in front of us, and we don't see it. It's obvious, but it takes someone else to point it out to us. It's like having a poppy seed stuck in your tooth. You can't see it, but when someone mentions it to you, you can feel it. You wonder, with a sinking feeling, how long it's been there.

So I'm wondering how many of you have been waiting for me to answer the obvious question that a dear friend posed to me this week. She wanted to know who or what my tiger is.

I tried to sidestep her question by suggesting that we all have tigers. You should know for yourself what yours is without my having to disclose my own. "Not so fast there," my friend said. So I will attempt to explain, beginning with a dream.

Lately my dreams have been undergoing a shift. For the most part, when I appear in them I am able-bodied. But from time to time now, I appear as I truly am these days—not so able-bodied. I am learning the language of my new body. I have always understood these dreams in a positive light. For me, they indicate a shift in consciousness, an expansion into a broader awareness, and also an acceptance of my life as it is, as I am actually living it. The wonderful thing about dreams is that they just are. What appears in dreams is neither good nor bad. It just is.

I often think dreams are my heart's way of presenting me with vital information in a form I can accept. So I have to honor the information I received from a recent dream. In it, I was dying. I was, very specifically, drawing my last breath. In the dream, I panicked, and when I woke up, the dream was still very present. My heart was racing, and I knew, beyond the shadow of a doubt, that I am not ready to die. Yet this is not what I've been telling myself and others for the past year or so.

From time to time since my ALS diagnosis, someone will ask me how I feel about dying. Consistently, my response has been: I'm not afraid of dying; it's the living that has me concerned. But now I know that that is simply not true. I'm afraid of it all—not just afraid—terrified. This is my tiger. I am petrified of the place where my body is taking me. I don't think there's anything unusual about this. It actually feels pretty normal.

Having felt abnormal for so much of my life, this element of normalcy is rather comforting, in a way. But not comforting enough. I live, I realize, in a state of persistent fear. I spend my days keeping it at bay. This is the tiger that stalks me, a part of myself that I keep as far away from me as possible. And, because I am here and the tiger is out there, I am not whole. The energy it takes to maintain two bodies, the one here and the one out there, is exhausting. No wonder I get so tired and angry. No wonder I feel such despair at times. Somehow, although it sounds counterintuitive to say this, I need to find a way to bring the tiger here to me. I need to be whole, and as long as the tiger is out there, I cannot be.

Thinking about this dilemma I am struck by the fact that in achieving wholeness, I will need to accomplish a new kind of separation. My fear now is entirely focused on the functioning of my body—I am afraid of living in it in the time ahead, and I'm afraid of separating from it in death. Somehow, though, I will need to fully embrace a new reality, still dim in my current awareness. I will need to learn that I am not my body.

I thought I already knew this. Years of studying the great spiritual teachings have taught me over and over that who we really are has nothing to do with flesh and blood. But as so often happens along the great path to knowledge, understanding something intellectually is not the same as truly knowing it. I'm always a little embarrassed when I discover how shallow my understanding is. Because I am blessed with a good mind, I understand lots of things I don't truly know. Ouch!

I think it's time to revisit some of the sages, mindful of my new context. Fear of death is such a magnificent motivator. It clears the mind with astounding thoroughness. I don't mean to sound ghoulish, but you might try it. Get a jump on things, as it were. After all, where I am is one of the great universal islands in the stream. We all visit it at some point, I think.

When someone asks me how the teachings of my meditation master have affected my life, an image immediately comes to me. I see myself walking into a familiar room. Until that moment, though, I have never stood in the room and simply looked around. Usually I just pop in and out. But now I am taking myself on a tour.

The room is very dark, so dark that the perimeters—floor, ceiling, and walls—are all in shadow. The only light comes from two sources: the doorway I have just walked through and a bright spot on one wall—not a window because the light is too diffuse. The edges of the room are filled with books containing all of the great spiritual teachings. Off to one side, near the light wall, sits a large, overstuffed chair. At the base of the light wall is a pool of liquid just large enough to submerge myself in, should I choose to do so. This room is where I go when I am searching for inner wisdom. It is very comfortable. I visit it often. I would like to live here, and I wonder whether, if I actually did live here, the darkness would resolve into some form of light.

The wisdom I am seeking, be it something I hold in my hand and read, or something I hold in my heart, is in this room. For the time being, it's just good to have a place to go. If you'd like to go with me, stay tuned.

All my love,
Catherine

15 July 2005

Dear Ones,

I've just had one of those exquisite moments of clarity. I feel better. Such a simple statement: I feel better. I realized it quite suddenly the other day. All at once, I was aware that the gloom had lifted. My mind has quieted. My heart feels light. It's as if this period of intense, unhappy struggle has formed a giant wave, and its power has deposited me on some new shore.

I always know when I have landed in a new place because I am aware that I'm thinking new thoughts, inviting new perspectives. (I don't know if this is true for you, but I am astounded by how much of my life I live on autopilot. I have certain set ways of responding to situations, and I go to that set response automatically.) One of the hallmarks of this "new place," however, is that for one, infinitesimal moment, time stops—just long enough for me to catch a glimpse of myself. In this moment, I see two things—how I usually respond, and the world of alternate possibilities. Being a curious sort of person, in the presence of something new and shiny, I feel an attraction. I look to the new, the next great adventure.

And so I found myself the other day suddenly aware that the ever present anguish and sadness I have felt since my return from India had lifted. The awareness came instantly, but the transformation did not. I know that it has been going on all this time. I have been like someone walking through a dark forest, taking a bend in the road and quite suddenly emerging into a sunny meadow. The meadow was there all along and I have been making my way toward it, but I couldn't see it until I was in it.

I know this experience. I have had it before, but never quite in this way. This time, and for the first time in my memory, I had a moment of absolute stillness that beckoned me to new awareness. In that moment, I had dual vision, like that of a split screen TV. On one side I saw my habitual response to a return to contentment following a period of discomposure: I braced for impact. Assuming this period of calm to be transitory, I quickly used it to prepare myself for the next, inevitable, blast of depression. I raced through the meadow consumed with anxious anticipation, devoted to the proposition that I must immediately reenter the dark forest.

But then there was the other screen presenting me with a beguiling alternative. While the first screen was all wordless anxiety and dread, this new one spoke to me. It said, quite simply, "Stay." This quiet command was mercifully followed by a few words of clarification, "You may be destined to return to the forest, but not right this minute. Right now, allow yourself to go deeply into this contentment. In this contentment lies the power that you will take with you the next time you enter the forest."

Always before, I have viewed contentment as something I could not bear to lose, and therefore could not bear to fully feel. It was a light state, insubstantial, unimportant, a delightful distraction from the serious business of life. Now I see contentment quite differently. It is true north, the magnetic pole that draws me, the star that guides me. If I can truly recognize its essence as my own, I can bring it with me no matter where I go. I had a moment in which I saw all of this, a moment before the fear set in.

How pesky this fear is! Just when I think everything is solid and moving splendidly, I am afraid. Of what? What could be fearful about contentment? It boggles the mind, or at least it boggles mine. Perhaps I am simply afraid of the unknown. After all, I've never really hung out in contentment before. Do I think that lying not far under its peaceful demeanor I will find . . . what? . . . tigers? Simple contentment cannot be trusted? Please note the exasperated tone with which I ask these questions.

But contentment ain't so simple. It requires discipline. Contentment and anxiety are a pair of wayward twins. Undisciplined, contentment breeds anxiety, even as anxiety longs for contentment. When I think of myself in a state of contentment, I imagine myself lying in a hammock, gently swaying in a warm summer breeze. Without warning, fear intercedes. It wants to tell me about all of the other things I should be doing, the "productive" thoughts I should be having, the regrettable consequences of taking this quiet time. My breathing shortens, my body stiffens, and the moment is lost. That's how fear works. But contentment is hard work, in its unique way.

But I like this work. Sometimes it takes me to the dark wisdom room I described in my last update. Sometimes, even better, it takes me nowhere at all.

Yesterday morning, I woke up aware that some of my anxiety and depression had returned. The signs are quite familiar. I become impatient with my physical limitations (yesterday's angry explosion involved throwing frozen food—very satisfying). Damning visions of future impairment claw at my mind. Inevitably, feelings of hopelessness and despair creep in. But this time, the visitation was short-lived. I knew something or someone would come my way to help restore my equilibrium. And so it was, via a timely call from a beloved friend whose contagious joy set me gently but firmly back in the meadow.

Recently I wrote to Dr. Joshi, to let him know that I was feeling better. It's hard to describe exactly what "feeling better" actually means. As my ALS symptoms continue to progress, it's not about relief from illness. My walking grows more labored. I tire easily. I fell the other day and bruised my ribs. Despite all this, I feel somehow stronger. I can't explain it any better than that.

We continue to get the house ready to be sold. For the last three weeks, Scott has been working solo on the outside. You should come and see it in its new red coat. It looks wonderful. I thought I might have to caution myself against falling in love with it all over again, as I did 30 years ago when I first saw it. But actually, I find myself delighted that new owners could not help but love this house as much as I have. I do look forward to the new adventure of our new home, wherever and whatever it may be.

Thanks to so many of you, large quantities of detritus have been sorted and removed from the house. We feel lighter by the day and look forward to the time when we can set out on the first actual house hunting expedition of our lives. As a friend who called this morning pointed out, "Your next house will be as perfect for you now as your current house was 30 years ago. It's just waiting for you to be ready for it."

On that happy note, I look forward to seeing many of you in the weeks ahead. Beware: anyone who visits us now gets put to work—it's a seven dwarfs kind of thing.

All my love,
Catherine

20 August 2005

Dear Ones,

Greetings, from the Land of Limbo! It's a challenge to write about a life in limbo, which is what mine currently feels like. This is why you haven't heard from me in a while—that and the fact that it's been just too bloody hot to think, much less write.

One of the many joys that Scott brought into my life was hiking in the Sierra Mountains. I came from one of those families that believed that "roughing it" was living in a house with only one bathroom. Scott introduced me to the captivating wonder of wandering in the great outdoors and sleeping (soundly) without a roof over my head, besotted by the beauty all around. In the Sierras, I saw clear rivers and streams that appeared placid on the surface but actually moved with astounding power below. I am reminded of them now.

On the surface, it seems that we have spent our summer preparing for things. Galen has been finishing off her last two undergraduate courses and preparing to take the MCATs (a marathon she is actually running as I write this). Owen has been settling into a new job and working all available networks to find his next gig—first choice, a small restaurant in the South of France. Scott has been working on the house and preparing to leave for Taiwan. I have been emptying the house in anticipation of a new home. Galen, it seems, is the only one of us on any kind of discernible timeline.

And yet, below the surface, things have been moving and are beginning to resolve—most notably, Taiwan, which was canceled about three weeks ago. Scott and I and our immediate and extended family (including many of you) greeted this news with mixed emotions. On the one hand, Scott will be here to participate in our move. On the other, it's a financial blow. Nonetheless, it's part of the powerful stream flowing under the placid surface. We are going somewhere new, and this is what it will take to get us there. In another week, the house will be ready to go. A wonderful young couple have expressed interest in it. If they are able to make an offer, then we can start looking. If not, the house will be on the market by the end of the month.

I realize that my sense of limbo has been exacerbated by the fact that I have spent my summer in a way quite different from the one I had planned. In my plan, Scott was leaving for Taiwan in June, and I was going to hit the road: Oregon, North Carolina, New Mexico, and points North. Well, I did get the "points North" part in: Maine with Eleanor and Jim, New Hampshire with Catharine, and Vermont with the sublime Mark and Geof. Thanks to all of them, and attendant guests, it has been a splendid summer.

The other thing that's in limbo, and probably always will be, is my sense of what I'm physically capable of doing. I try to guess, but past experience, even recent past experience, is not much of a guide. So some days, I try to do more than I actually can, and end up with a broken rib, as I did about six weeks ago when I fell trying to move a flower box. And some days, I decide there are things I can no longer do, and then discover that I'm being premature. Needless to say, I much prefer the latter experience, but even the former reminds me of how healthy I still am—6 weeks later, the rib is fully healed.

So I'm dancing along that thin line—taking small risks, determined to keep myself active, and maintaining an open but watchful mind. It was in honoring this dance that I discovered I can still swim. Because cold tends to leach the strength out of my muscles, I had assumed that it was no longer safe to go swimming, something I have always loved. But there I was, at a beautiful lake in Maine, with two strong and determined women who announced that if I would try, they would save me—if need be. Perhaps it was just the intriguing picture of them saving me, but a few moments later I found myself with a piece of foam tubing across my chest.

I kicked off into the water and swam, and swam, and swam. No saving needed, just the glorious feeling of moving through water with the strength and freedom I no longer experience on land. It was heaven! Earlier this week, I visited this heaven once again—a plunge into the Connecticut River with five stalwart men in attendance (I'm always reminding Galen that she may be a princess, but I am the queen—5 men, indeed!). The key, of course, is warm water.

I've entered a new drug trial, an investigation into whether CoQ10, in large doses, will slow down my symptoms. This being a trial, there's always the possibility that I'm taking a placebo (as was, in fact, the case in my last trial). But this, too, is part of the dance. I will also see Dr. Joshi at the end of the month. I have just received, through the good graces of someone who went to Nagpur in July, the most astounding package of new syrups and herbs from Mukul. Dr. Joshi is not giving up. Neither am I, although I have not been quite the loyal basti Queen he had hoped for this summer. We do what we can.

And . . . mark your calendars. On September 18th, which is a Sunday, we'll be participating in the Melville-Park neighborhood yard sale. It's a huge, multi-block extravaganza. All of those things that have left our house already or are soon to leave will find their way onto the lawn at Centerville Park, a couple of blocks from our house. Come one, come all! Bring cash! My sisters will be here, Owen and Galen will be on hand, Scott will be lurking. It should be fun.

And that, from the Land of Limbo, is the tiny landmark we are using to steady ourselves as we move forward. Join us.

All my love,
Catherine

8 September 2005

Dear Ones,

The night I arrived in Nagpur, I lay down on my bed and these thoughts ambled into my brain: "What on earth am I doing? I am thousands of miles from home. I am alone in a strange country where I don't speak the language or know the customs. And I can't even walk! What was I thinking?" Shortly thereafter, mercifully, jet lag overcame me and I fell asleep. But before I did, I had a moment in which I felt genuinely unnerved and very exposed. There have been other times, especially during the dislocations of my peripatetic youth, when I had similar feelings. But nothing prepared me for the gut-wrenching feeling of having someone pound a "For Sale" sign into the ground in front of my house.

At moments like these I have a visceral understanding of how wholly inadequate the mind is. I have no doubt that moving to a new house is absolutely for the best. My heart, however, remains unconvinced. I am at cross purposes with myself, my mind focused on the future and on "moving toward," my heart focused on loss. There's room for both, but right now my heart has the upper edge because its concern is something tangible: leaving our house. So I know what I'm leaving, but I don't know what I'm moving toward. That's a pretty tidy statement about life, isn't it? I don't know when I became so fearful, but I'm glad to have an opportunity to see its face. I suppose that this has something to do with tigers.

The details of the sale of our house are in good hands. Our broker is knowledgeable and compassionate and is moving quickly. Because some of this process in recent weeks has felt a lot like pulling a Band-Aid off slowly, we are very happy to have her expertise and enthusiasm on our side. For all our sakes, we need to move with dispatch.

Even Dr. Joshi, when I saw him last week, encouraged us to be expeditious. Remember those three aspects, or in the language of ayurveda, "doshas" of the body: vata, pitta, and kapha? A year ago, all of my doshas were elevated. By the time I left Nagpur, kapha had reached an optimal level, and pitta was greatly reduced. Vata, my major issue, had also shown improvement. When I saw Dr. Joshi in May, things were holding steady. But when I saw him last week, my vata had started to edge back up. One of the chief culprits is stress—physical and emotional. Also, I have discovered recently that I am currently anemic (something I have had to manage most of my adult life). And, in the last three months I have lost 10 pounds. So, stress and fatigue . . . . not a happy combination. But I'm reminded that this combination affects healthy people's vatas, too.

Dr. Joshi was by no means doom and gloom, however. In fact, quite the opposite. He is always reminding me that opportunities for health abound. From his perspective, as long as my vital organs are sound, which they manifestly continue to be, he sees opportunities and hope. On a day-to-day basis, I see diminished physical capacity. But he sees the world through another lens. He always explains things carefully and clearly, and I come away with renewed awareness of my body's fundamental strength. That alone is an incalculable blessing. He has added a few calories to my diet, and I'm taking an iron supplement. We talked about the advisability of my returning to Nagpur in January. At this point, he feels optimistic, but he wants to wait to see me again in November before making a final decision. I would love to go again, as would Scott. In a strange and wonderful way, it was one of the most sublime times we have ever spent together.

Things are moving on the homefront: Owen and Galen are now happily ensconced in their new apartments. We have given the piano away to a family with children. Last night I had the giddy pleasure of watching it being rolled up the street to its new home. For a few minutes, someone actually played it as it sat on the sidewalk in front of our house. Later, one of the children came down to thank me. We have had one open house, and another one is scheduled this weekend. My beloved sisters will be arriving soon to help with the yard sale, and I know that my dear, saintly friend Sarah is looking forward to getting her living room back.

Moving seems such a test of faith, and I am humbled and a little appalled to see the limits of my faith so near. But Scott said something last night that has, at least for now, aligned my heart and my mind. He reminded me of the simple fact that in order to receive something new, our hands must be empty. We have to put down what we have held in our hands for so long, to prepare to receive the blessings to come. For me, that is one magnificent thought.

All my love,
Catherine

26 September 2005

Dear Ones,

This morning I drove out of town with the Sheriff on my tail. There she was, in a big, brown van following me up Talbot, right on Blue Hill, left on American Legion. Whew! No posse, just "the *wo*man." (In Boston, our Sheriff is Andrea Cabral.) It made me think about the nature of paranoia and those other blights on the human spirit: superstition, worry, guilt, shame.

I don't think much about these psychic gremlins when I live my days under the bright illusion that I am in control. This, even when I really haven't a clue what's coming up next—now there's a truly divine dance. The size of my dance partner changes daily. Sometimes I dance with a giant. I get a crick in my neck just trying to look him in the eye. Other times, I am reminded of when I used to dance with my small son, his feet on top of my feet as we whirled giggling around the room.

So I write you now in the midst of the dance. The yard sale is, mercifully, over. Goodwill made out like a bandit. 100 years (Or *is it only 30?*) of National Geographics have gone to an art therapy program in Connecticut. And the books—all those books!—have gone to a library in central Massachusetts. As for the rest of us, we're just happy it's over.

We have now had two open houses. Ignore the newspapers, and all the prophets of doom. We have had many visitors. As yet, however, no one has left a check on the kitchen table. Our house is so unnaturally clean it's even creeping the dog out. And the stress of keeping such a clean house . . . Oh, my God! It's just not—how you say?—*me*.

One thing you may have noticed about Dr. Joshi is that he likes metaphors. After all, I would not own not just one but two copies of "Little Black Sambo" if it were not for his tiger metaphor last May. (I'm still mulling the significance of the reemergence of this story in my life. When I first read it—or, actually, had it read to me—I was a young colonial lass, age six, living in Singapore, an irony not at all lost on me now.) But Dr. Joshi's lively mind is not content to rest in a single metaphor. So in August, he had a new one.

When he listens to my pulses, everything seems to stop. Even in noisy Nagpur, absolute silence reigns. He hears the world through his fingertips, my world. Then he interprets it for me. Last month, the world he heard was at war. Those were his words. A battle is raging between my natural and strong ability to heal and the forces of the imbalance in my system that we call ALS. Remember Dr. Sathe, Dr. Joshi's mentor? He called Dr. Joshi in July to ask about my progress. He believes that if I am to experience any positive response to the treatment, it will probably be during this upcoming month, October. So the time is at hand, the combatants are engaged. I do feel a little bit like Arjuna in the chariot with Krishna, trying to understand and act upon my correct role.

I'm taking my herbs. I am meditating and doing breathing exercises. I am adhering to the diet as closely as I can, given the limitations of time, energy, and the realities of family life. A bout of anemia and several weeks of debilitating neck pain (I must have been dancing with that giant!) have temporarily curtailed my hatha yoga workout. Scott, bless him, gives me thrice-weekly ayurveda massages. And, I'm sure you will all be deliriously happy to learn, I am once again the Basti Queen of 1 Larchmont Street. But even more, I am aware of and rest securely in the downy nest of prayers and blessings I am offered on a daily basis.

Every time Scott and I tell someone new that our house is on the market, the first question they ask is "Where are you going?" Again and again, we hear ourselves saying "We don't know." There are days when the greatest gift I can give myself is the physical reminder that I stand on solid ground, no matter where I am, and no matter what size my dance partner is. I'm sure that's why "laying on of hands" has become so important to me. Everything from simple hugs to Nicole's cranio-sacral work serves to remind me that wherever I am, I am home.

And speaking of homes, here is what we are looking for: most, or all, of the living space on one floor, and a two-car garage attached to a workshop. This could be a ranch house with garage and workshop in the basement. Or it could be a cape with the master bedroom on the first floor and a separate garage onto which a workshop could be built. Or even be the first floor of a two-family house. I'm sure there are other permutations as well, but this is as far as my imagination can go right now. You know, you can't have if you don't ask.

We haven't actually started looking for the new house yet. We're not in a position to buy a house until this house is sold, and I am doing my best not to drive myself crazier than I already am. This, these days, is what passes for wisdom. For more on the whole house thing, see below.

Next up? A change in mobility. Stay tuned.

All my love,
Catherine

CARRY THE ONE

From time to time, I write to you about a subject that I want to pursue more deeply. It's like when you're adding a column of figures and the resulting number is too large for that column. You have to "carry the one."

Such is the case with what I refer to as "the house thing." For the last couple of years I have belonged to a writers group. As any of you who have ever belonged to such a group know, membership requires discipline. Once a month, I have to write something. Naturally, I'm inclined to write about whatever is foremost on my mind at the time. This past week, I wrote a piece about my house.

I am standing on the porch of the house. Wooden planks creak under my feet. The land falls away from the house so abruptly I feel like I'm on a stage. I'm standing on the part of the porch that arcs out around the bay windows. My eyes are closed. I can smell the sea. In years to come, my ability to smell the ocean from this porch will mean everything.

Behind me, bay windows, in fact all of the windows in the house, are covered by gray boards. The gray boards are covered with black graffiti. Sumac trees grow up through the fieldstone foundation. Former residents have scratched their names through the varnish in the front door. On the other side of the door, a guard dog barks with fierce intention, effectively keeping us outside on this cold March day.

A few days later, the dog will be escorted to a waiting van; and we will tour the house, walking through the unnatural midday darkness of a house with boarded windows, illuminated by high-powered fluorescent flashlights. We will see that the house has no plumbing. Scavengers have removed all the copper pipes. We will see that many of the windows are broken, including what must once have been a large stained-glass window in the front stairwell. Vandals have had their way. The house has no electricity. For some unknown reason, the cable out to the street has been severed. We will smell that the guard dog never goes outside. We will see the collapsed ceiling and the fire-blackened corner in the kitchen. The mantel that belongs in the family room is resting precariously against a wall in the dining room, its beveled mirror broken.

We will see all of this and not turn away. The smell of the sea is in our nostrils and works its olfactory magic on our perceptions. Through the grime and destruction, somehow we see the glory. Somehow, we see our future, bright and compelling. Through the early years this vision is challenged constantly.

We have decided to settle in Dorchester, Massachusetts, in 1977, amid the street gangs, the abandoned houses, the vacant lots, and packs of feral dogs. I still remember my suburban parents coming for their first visit. I hear my mother's voice before she is even out of the car. She is speaking to my father in an unnaturally loud and high-pitched voice: "This isn't so bad, Scottie. This isn't so bad, Scottie. This isn't it so bad, Scottie." Over and over, all the way up the front walk. My father, for his part, simply offers to buy me a gun for my upcoming birthday.

I later learn that a distant forbear lived in Dorchester in the 18th-century—a fascinating but ultimately useless pedigree against the realities of 20th-century urban life. Nonetheless, this is what we want. We move in the week before Labor Day. With bold ignorance, we move in before the electricity has been restored. We are in the middle of a heat wave and, without electricity, have no recourse to fans. Innocently, as the long Labor Day weekend approaches, I call the city Inspectional Services Department to ask for the permit required to perform the work. The man from the city tells me it will be weeks before a permit can be approved. I think ahead to untold weeks without the security and comfort of lights after dark, never mind the fans. I threaten hell and damnation, doing my best imitation of "woman on the verge of a nervous breakdown," and he relents. Later I am told I have worked a miracle. The man was looking for a bribe, but agreed to issue the permit without one. Ignorance is, once again, truly bliss.

In the first few years, we are robbed and mugged. Somehow, we are undamaged. We become street smart. The houses around us fill up with new people. We bond with our neighbors. Soon the only dogs we see are leashed to people carrying plastic bags. Two years after we arrive, after 36 hours of labor, much of it spent soaking in the clawfoot tub in the upstairs bathroom, our son Owen is born in the bedroom at the front of the house over the big bay window. In another three years, after watching the sunrise through the upstairs sitting room window that offers a panoramic view of the neighborhood, our daughter Galen is born in the same bedroom.

Still later, my baby sister will marry her true love within the embrace of the big bay window. The dining room will host innumerable extended family dinners around the table especially made in Hong

Kong—including Thanksgivings so large a second table has to be added. It will also host the meals that follow the funerals of both of my parents.

Time and hard work heal the house's wounds. New windows, plumbing, electricity, roof, shingles, paint, and more paint, and more paint. A deck is added off the back. The neighborhood has changed. Now we can sit out at night and enjoy the sounds around us without fear. Where once we closed ourselves in after dark, now we sit and enjoy the fall serenade of cicadas.

Black-and-white photographs show the house as we first saw it. To love this house at first sight might defy the laws of gravity. I look at these photographs now and remember how hollow and foreign it once seemed. We had moved from a two-bedroom apartment. For a long time, we had whole rooms that had no furniture. Voices and footfalls echoed sharply off the walls. Our children could play soccer indoors. But slowly, without our really being aware of it, it filled up.

Now, the echoes have returned. At first I thought my heart would break at the prospect of leaving a place I loved so well. But the heart is too optimistic, practical, and robust for that. As the process of transition continues, the clearing out and giving away of things no longer needed, the cleaning, the painting, the realtor's rituals, closure begins. The heart expands to embrace the new. The echoes remind me of all that has been, and confirm that it was good.

In 1977, after a lifetime of wandering, I went looking for a home, and one was given to me. So it will be again.

30 October 2005

Dear Ones,

Asking for and accepting help have never been my strong suit. Like many of us, I am far more comfortable giving help than receiving it. Strangely enough, in the past year or so, I have found that this inhibition extends even to inanimate objects. Go figure!

As with so many things, necessity and practice have trumped reluctance. Now, I don't mind asking for an arm to hold as I make my way across the room, or two strong hands to open that pesky jar, or a gadget or two that make life seem normal. To that end, I began using voice recognition software with my computer late last spring. Every update I have sent you since then has been "spoken" rather than typed. Did you notice? In my mind, my writing style changes. How I speak is not necessarily how I write. I could be wrong about this.

But change has been gradual. For the most part, it has seeped into my life in a quiet and unassuming way. One day, I acknowledge that I need the support, and it is there. Case in point, last spring I noticed that I was becoming reluctant to leave the house. It had happened so gradually that at first I wasn't aware. Then one day, I needed some basil from the garden. I immediately found myself negotiating with the recipe. Perhaps I could simply do without. But, traditional pesto without basil? I even thought of changing the menu. But at that point I brought myself up short. What on earth was the problem here? And then I realized that a pattern had been forming. I was becoming like an old dog that hadn't left the sunny spot on the porch for days. The reason became obvious.

Our house is perched on the side of a hill, resulting in a high foundation. The high foundation necessitates three sets of very steep stairs. Until this summer, none of the staircases had railings. Gradually my ability to navigate these stairs has waned. The tumble off the stairs that resulted in a broken rib added to my timidity. I needed those railings! I told Scott and, voilà!, railings. The addition of three modest railings was the equivalent of a three-day pass. Whoopee!

I learned from the railings experience how quickly I am willing to limit my horizons unnecessarily. Without even thinking about it, I had simply lowered my expectations. I did it the same thing before using voice recognition software. For a time, because typing was so difficult, I simply stopped writing altogether. Imagine! It was during that period just after my return from India. I kept putting off composing updates. But these two examples are minor compared with one area I have treated with obstinacy.

In order to walk safely on two feet, I now wear substantial plastic braces on the lower half of both legs. The braces are clumsy and awkward and a bit heavy. My walking style reminds me of the character Lurch from "The Addams Family." Around Halloween, and with my arms extended above my head, my hands making claws, I am capable of terrorizing small children with my monster imitation.

Like everything else, I came to the braces only after several falls had convinced me I needed them. My legs have become quite thin, and they tire easily. These days, they are like an SUV with a two-gallon gas tank.

But I am stubborn, and I want to walk. For months now, if I couldn't walk, I wouldn't go. As with the railings, my obstinacy was once again imprisoning me. The answer, of course, was for me to get a wheelchair—and use it. My friend Chris, who got over his own wheelchair phobia more than thirty years ago, was kindly waiting in the wings. From time to time, he would raise the issue gently with me, and then, with the deftness of a fencing master, drop it—only to raise it again a few months later. Then, one day in August, I realized there was something I wanted to do but would not be able to do if I had to walk. I called Chris, and a week later he appeared at my door with a shiny, red wheelchair.

The chair was wheeled into my kitchen, and Chris invited me to sit in it. Then the two of us sat there, Chris in his chair and I in mine, and he introduced me to this new world. And once again, with a sigh of deep relief, I felt my world expand. A month later, I was loading my chair onto an airplane. Because of the chair, I was able to see as much of beautiful Santa Fe as I wanted to. I was surprised to realize how much of my time had been spent looking for a wall to lean against or a bench to sit on. In his quiet way, Chris has also been preparing me for the psychology of using a wheelchair. It is true that a wheelchair has the most amazing effect on able-bodied people. For better or worse (and it's not all bad), wheelchair users do become invisible.

Just to give you an idea of how stubborn I am and how long it takes me to comprehend the obvious, I actually took my first wheelchair ride a year ago. The story of that ride is in "Carry the One," below. It took me from that time until now to complete a journey from total denial to wary acceptance. But the good news is the acceptance was not begrudging. As I was wheeling around Santa Fe last year, I was aware of how grateful I was to be out in the general populace doing what people do. But when Scott went to take a photograph of me sitting in my chair, I waved him away with: "I'm not ready yet"

In a way it is laughable that I resist help when I most need it. But as I move into each new level of physical disability, it seems natural to resist. Also, it seems healthy to do so. I prefer to focus on the health of the situation, not the dis-ease. And despite recent changes, I still persist in feeling very healthy, and, I'm told, looking healthy as well. I haven't lost any more weight. My energy level is unpredictable, but I move through each day feeling strong and optimistic.

What am I optimistic about? It does seem irrational, but life is good, and my life is filled with a quality I can only describe as grace.

My love to you all,
Catherine

CARRY THE ONE
Sit in the Chair (December 2004)

She was waiting for me when I got off the plane. A lovely young woman, a blue head scarf completely covering her hair. I could hardly look her in the eye. This was an encounter I had been dreading, as much for its import as for its inevitability. I struggled to greet her courteously. It wasn't her fault. I wonder if she noticed my deep intake of breath as I asked her, "Is that for me?"

If she noticed, she was too polite to show it. She simply glanced at the walkie-talkie attached to her belt and answered my question with a question. "Are you Catherine Royce?" It was like that moment when the new dentist, who is meeting you for the first time, calls your name.

For an instant, it crossed my mind to say no, and to postpone the experience. But I knew that delay was not an option. The time had come. Necessity required that I submit, with as much dignity as I could summon, to this next step in the gradual and seemingly inexorable loss of my cherished sense of self-sufficiency: the wheelchair.

How many times, I wondered, had this young woman seen this moment of hesitation? How many times had she seen someone take a deep breath and bow her head to this necessity? How many times had she been the one to offer someone that first reluctantly taken ride?

My first wheelchair ride was deeply instructive. A friend had suggested it might be fun. It was not fun—at least not at first. I saw the young woman standing there with the chair. It was open and waiting for me. As I had walked from the plane, I had been talking with an attractive man my own age. That did not help my situation. I had to break off my conversation with him abruptly. He did, of course, notice. Not only was I having to do this, sit in the chair, but I was having to do it in public. I imagined myself in his eyes, going in the blink of an eye from being a striking middle-aged woman to being a cripple—from being an person of interest to being an object of concern or even pity.

There was no real way to prepare myself for the onslaught of feelings. The decision had been made quite suddenly. That morning, as I prepared to leave for the airport, my traveling companion had phoned. A court case she had been trying had suddenly gone awry, and she needed to stay to attend to it. I would have to fly alone.

Fly alone. There was a time in my not-too-distant past when I flew alone two or three times a week. I liked to fly alone. Actually, I preferred it. But that was before ALS weakened my legs and made my hands clumsy. Suddenly, I felt less confident in my ability to take care of myself. Suddenly, I had to ask for help. In this new role as help-receiver, instead of my accustomed role of help-giver, I hardly knew myself. I felt raw and exposed. I didn't like it—not a bit.

But it never crossed my mind to cancel my trip. Instinctively and immediately, I knew there had to be another solution. My logical mind found one before my ego had a chance to assess the consequences and cancel. As I checked in for the flight that morning, I asked myself a simple question: "How far apart are the gates when I change planes in Detroit, and how much time do I have to make the change?"

No sooner had I thought the question, than it came out of my mouth to the ticket agent. She looked up at me when she gave the answer, saw my cane, and asked "Would you like help?" Again, my fearless logic answered: "Yes," I said. And that was that. I walked onto the plane in Boston and put the consequences of my decision out of my mind.

But when I got off the plane in Detroit, there she was—the lovely young woman with the hideous chair. I was assailed by emotions, mostly horrific, but they all boiled down to one over-arching thought. By walking up to the wheelchair and sitting down, I was crossing a line, walking through a one-way mirror. On one side of the mirror, I was a strong, able-bodied woman. On the other side, I was a genderless cripple. On one side, I was a whole, competent, imposing woman. On the other side, I simply disappeared.

I could feel my shallow breathing, feel myself controlling panic. My humiliation was palpable, and I did not want anyone to know it. And then something happened (which a friend of mine who has used a wheelchair all of his adult life later confirmed for me): I disappeared in plain sight. But I didn't hate this strange metamorphosis as I thought I would. This disappearing—unique to people with noticeable handicaps—is really quite wonderful. There I was, sitting miserably in a wheelchair, convinced that I was the object of pity and derision from every eye when, in fact, every eye was turned to look everywhere but at me. No one was looking. The wheelchair was like my own private little room.

All of this happened in the time it took to roll up the jetway. By the time we reached the gate, new sensations were emerging. Invisible, I could look around. My wheelchair attendant wanted to know where I needed to go, and all sorts of impish responses suggested themselves: Cancun, a nice bed-and-breakfast in the Pyrenees, my brother's house in Oregon. But I confined myself to a stop to purchase lunch before going to my next gate. I was in good hands, in every way. She was efficient, gracious, and solicitous. If I had to cross this terrible divide, she was the perfect companion. I wondered if doing this job had taught her compassion or if she had come to it already well endowed.

At the next airport, new wheelchair adventures awaited. Yes, now it was an adventure. By the time I got off the plane in Albuquerque, I can't say I was looking forward to my next ride, but I was more cheerfully resigned to it. And sensing my blossoming confidence, the gods sent me comic relief. My maiden ride had been with the essence of serenity. For my very next ride, I had a cowboy. A real cowboy.

"Howdy, Ma'am, my name is J.C.," he said as we rolled up the jetway. Out at the gate, he pulled me up alongside an elderly woman, also sitting in a wheelchair. We greeted each other. For a moment, I wondered if I also looked elderly, and then remembered I was invisible, and it didn't matter. "Ready?" he asked enthusiastically, and at that moment I realized he was going to push us both at once. Suddenly, I felt like a baby in a double stroller. Unhappiness started to rise in my throat. But J.C. was so aggressively cheerful he rocked me right out of myself. Also, he pushed both chairs at such a high rate of speed, I knew that anyone seeing us, especially any children seeing us, would be filled with envy. This was fun. YEEE HAAA!!!

And just when I thought this couldn't get any better, a relative of the elderly woman appeared, taking over the pushing of her chair, and J.C. kicked mine into an even higher gear. Suddenly, I was transported to another place and time. I was on a street in Indonesia. Scott and I were bumping along in a bechak—a pedicab—with our driver pedaling behind us at breakneck speed. The colors, smells, and sights of that exotic land whirled past us. We were giddy with the sensations of it all. And here I was now, on my way to the baggage claim area at the Albuquerque International Airport, giddy all over again. And giddy even more when I found myself sitting in my hotel room. I had successfully traveled, by myself. I could still do this! I had crossed over into new territory, but that's the joy of life. Do I dread the day when the wheelchair becomes a constant companion? Of course, I do. But for now, a frontier has been put behind me. I walked across it and sat down; the world kept moving, and I kept moving with it.

CATHERINE ROYCE

14 November 2005

Dear Ones,

No sooner had we settled back into Boston after our trip to New Mexico, than Scott was gone. It's a little difficult to say where he is now and not sound like I'm trying to be funny. He is in Iraq. I'm not kidding. He left on November 5th and will be gone at least until Christmas. What on earth has possessed him to go to Iraq now? Well, cold cash, for one. Adventure, for another. This is how he makes his living. He is a government contractor, using his skills as a geologist to investigate the viability of building sites for mortar-proof shelters. In the time ahead, it will become increasingly difficult for him to be able to be away like this; so I wholeheartedly encouraged him to go. Well, "wholehearted" might be stretching things a little. Let's just say he went with my blessing.

In the nine days he has been gone, it has been instructive to see how dependent I have become on him, and by extension therefore, how dependent I now am. It happened so gradually that I was not really aware of it; I was under an illusion of independence. It's not that I can't do things for myself—I can. It's just that things take longer and I need to do them very, very carefully. But wait, I must be honest. There are, indeed, things I cannot do for myself. Small things: I can do the grocery shopping, but I can't get the groceries from the car into the house. I can wash the clothes, but I can't get them back upstairs. I can cook for myself, but I can't push a vacuum cleaner. If the lid the sticks on the jar, I must have something else for lunch. My day is like Swiss cheese—good solid material with a few holes.

As much as the prospect of being alone in the future fills me with dread, this is not such a time. The primary reason is that I am not, in fact, alone much. Our friend Paul has been staying with us for the past few weeks and will continue to do so for the foreseeable future. And Sarah—what more can I say about the formidable friendship my beloved Sarah bestows on me? When she heard Scott was going away, she immediately assembled a group of local ladies, longtime neighbors, to act as my support network. She calls it Catherine's Support, which I mightily restrain myself from referring to as Catsup. Oh, that is so bad!

So I am well cared for, and I know it. In fact, I went away this past weekend to New Hampshire and forgot to tell folks where I was going. Panic ensued. On the one hand, I'm dependent. On the other hand, I can't seem to remember that I am. My life is thus a study in contradictions, a play of opposites.

Speaking of opposites, lately my body has displayed its inconsistencies again. Recently, I pulled a muscle in my back. It healed. So why is my body willing and able to heal some things and not others? Some have suggested that perhaps ALS is an indication that the body's natural ability to heal has been overwhelmed. But if that's the case, how can it be so selective, healing some things quickly and other things not at all? Perhaps my body doesn't know something is amiss. If that were the case, how could I tell it? What would I need to do? How do I tap myself on the shoulder and say, "By the way, it might interest you to know that your nervous system is out of whack"? I'm pondering this at the moment. I think it probably has to do with coming to terms with tigers.

After reading my tiger contemplations earlier this year, a friend sent me Yann Martel's *Life of Pi*. In it, the protagonist is faced with the need to tame an actual tiger. He asks himself a series of questions: Does he have the time? Does he have the resolve? Does he have the knowledge? Is the reward great enough? I ask myself these same questions. The answer is yes, to all of them. Somehow, I think there's a relationship between my speaking to myself clearly and honestly and being able to unlock the secret of my illness. Of course, I could be skipping merrily down the wrong track. But it's worth pursuing. It is a little like being in a maze—going down a long path, only to discover a need to be willing to double back at a dead-end. It's also a bit like Hansel and Gretel following shiny pebbles in the moonlight. I have the time. I have the resolve. I have some knowledge and access to more. The reward is certainly great enough.

And it looks like I will be contemplating these things here at 1 Larchmont Street for a while longer. By some sublime quirk, we put our house on the market at exactly the most inopportune time. Never, in all the years I have lived here, has so much real estate in our neighborhood been on the market concurrently. (Our realtor has done her best, of this I have no doubt. But it's as though a group of us, who have all been neighbors for many years, became old and/or infirm on the same darn day.) So clearly, Scott and I are supposed to spend this winter sitting tight. In a week, we will take the house off the market until spring. I thought I might find this distressing after all the preparations for selling, but in fact I am mildly relieved. I could stay or go; but the prospect of a midwinter move feels daunting. We look to the spring.

And what of Dr. Joshi? Well, he will not be coming to Boston this month as he had planned; circumstances require his presence in Albuquerque. He has advised me not to try to come out to see him, but to talk to him on the telephone. We are in the process of arranging that now. Will I be going to India? Do I even want to go to India? I think the answer to the second question is yes. My trip last February/March was part one of a two-part process. If I do not go to India again, I will never know the full benefit of Ayurveda. However, Dr. Joshi may feel that the taxing nature of the travel would outweigh the benefits. We shall see.

I wish you all a bountiful Thanksgiving. Mine will be filled with family. It is—as I know it is for many of you—my favorite holiday.

All my love,
Catherine

9 December 2005

Dear Ones,

A friend of a friend sent me this story a few days ago:

Two Wolves

One evening an old Cherokee told his grandson about a battle that goes on inside people. He said, "My son, the battle is between two wolves inside us all. One is Evil. It is anger, envy, jealousy, sorrow, regret, greed, arrogance, self-pity, guilt, resentment, inferiority, false pride, superiority, and ego. The other is Good. It is joy, peace, love, hope, serenity, humility, kindness, benevolence, empathy, generosity, truth, compassion and faith."

The grandson thought about it for a minute and then asked his grandfather: "Which wolf wins?"

The old Cherokee replied, "The one you feed."

~ Cherokee legend

The eloquence of this story speaks for itself. My beast might be different; replace wolves with tigers. Nonetheless, I know the evil and court the good. In order to feed either, food must be near at hand. I don't know why the Twinkies I feed the evil seem so much more readily available than the organic tofu I need to nourish the good.

As you all know, the last time I wrote I was preparing to speak with Dr. Joshi on the telephone. That call happened ten days ago. It has taken me this long to fully understand what he said to me, and why, and how I feel about it. He asked me his usual litany of questions—about every thing from the steadiness of my mind to the temperature of my legs. In the end, he determined that I should not come to India anytime in the near future.

At this point, he feels that the continuing and increasing weakness I'm experiencing indicates that either his treatment will take longer than he had thought, or simply isn't working. In either case, he feels that the travel, alone, would be debilitating. But even without the travel, he does not feel that my body could withstand the rigors of panchakarma.

One of the things that I treasure in my relationship with Dr. Joshi is his total compassionate honesty. He has never held out false hope. He told me from the very beginning that his treatment was experimental—exactly like the drug trials I have been participating in here in Boston. (Well, not exactly, but you know what I mean.) I argued with him. I was willing to throw myself into whatever the next encounter might be. To this he said: "Yes, I know. You are doing your job. My job is to be the doctor." In this case, his job is to protect me from the more impetuous aspect of my nature. Of course, I know he's right.

And how do I feel about this? Surprisingly calm. In preparing myself for my conversation with him, I envisioned him giving me this news; in this vision, I found it upsetting. The reality is actually quite different. While I am indeed disappointed, I am not dismayed; nor do I feel despair. Part of me is, in fact, relieved. I know how weak I am. I know how easily I tire now. If he had told me to come to India, I would have gone in a heartbeat. I would have trusted that despite the demands of the journey, everything would be taken care of, just as it has been all along. There was a particular charm to the last trip to India. Without it, the trip might have been devastating.

I am aware now, as I think I was not before, that the ayurvedic treatment has been a success from the very beginning. Granted, it has not managed to curtail or even slow my symptoms. But it has given me something far more valuable: it has acted like an astral booster shot. I am mentally, emotionally, and spiritually stronger now than I was a year ago.

Does this mean that Dr. Joshi and I have finished our work together? At least for now, no. He is sending me a new protocol of herbs, and we are scheduled to check in again by phone in February. At that time, I will envy him his location. He will be back at that wonderful clinic I love so well. He will be listening to the mad cacophony of sound out on High Court Road. He will be enveloped by the gentle and perpetual presence of the divine that is his normal day. He will be in the company of some of the most loving people I have ever met. And not to put too fine a point on it, he will be in warm India and I will still be in chilly New England.

Nonetheless, we will speak, and I look forward to the sound of his voice, the truth of his wisdom, and the touch of his compassion. No matter what he has to say to me, he always leaves me feeling whole. He is truly the doctor.

And what of Scott? There was a time during his 30 year career of global travel, when he would leave Boston and I would not hear from him again until his return several months later. Once when he was doing a project in Nigeria, we devised a way to exchange audiotapes with each other. At the time, that was the height of communications savvy. Now, however, we have both e-mail and cell phone. One way or another, we are able to speak with each other almost daily. He has had some magical and some hair-raising experiences already. I am saving his e-mails because they tell such a great story. And because of our steady communication, I know that he is also relieved by Dr. Joshi's decision. He would never have told me not to go, but he also felt the enormity of the risk.

A few years ago, three dear friends and I spent some time contemplating our futures. We distilled our ruminations down to four simple statements. One of us wanted to own a small store. One of us wanted to run his own consulting business. One of us wanted to own an inn. And I wanted to go to India. Now, five years later, each of us has achieved our goal. The power of intention!

What is my intention now? To live my life fully and with complete faith that everything, *everything*, is for the best. As often as I can remember, this intention is what I feed my tiger. My assignment is to remember this more and more. When I first started contemplating the whole notion of a tiger, I didn't understand that in order even to have a tiger, you have to feed it. If you don't feed it, it will die, and you'll lose everything, the good and evil.

I closed a recent update with the comment that I felt my life was filled with grace. I'll have to admit it was kind of a toss off, the way to close a letter with a sort of "Amen." What do I mean by grace? In this context, grace is consistent memory. When my mind wants to feed the evil, consistent memory intercedes with food for the good.

I recently had lunch with a friend who asked me about my intention. Not content with a quick and superficial response, she probed. Through her systematic and loving questions, she led me down a path to realization. More and more now, my adventures, my travels, will take this form: internal, intense, focused, revealing and, I hope, deeply satisfying. To see more of the path revealed to me in this conversation, see "Carry the One" below.

In Scott's absence, I have been cradled in the abundant care of Sarah and her support group. I cannot begin to thank them for the sense of security and well-being with which they bless me. Dianne set the tone for this group. A few days before Scott left, it was predicted that we would have snow. Dianne made the following observation: "Scott isn't going to Iraq. He's going to New Mexico. You need help not because you can't take care of yourself. You just need to see your friends more often. And it is not going to snow tomorrow." To this day, I like Dianne's world best. That's my story, and I'm sticking to it.

All my love,
Catherine

Carry the One
Río Grande Gorge

Twenty years ago, I stood at the edge of the Rio Grande Gorge, confused and awed. It comes upon one like an optical illusion. As one approaches it, flat tableland as far as the eye can see, is broken only by the suggestion of mountains in the far distance. There is not even a hint that the land will suddenly fall away thousands of feet to the river below, until you're standing at the precipice. The sense of vertigo is immediate and intense. It literally took my breath away.

There are moments in our lives when an experience is so profound it seems to alter the very chemistry of our bodies. This is what it was like for me standing at the edge of Río Grande Gorge. Later, when I revisited the gorge in my imagination, I experienced the same visceral response. The first time this happened was while I watched "Thelma and Louise." Their car was perched on the edge of the gorge, and I was right there with them.

My most recent visit to the gorge, though, was in a dream. In the dream, I am once again standing at the edge. I have been running across the mesa and suddenly come to the precipice. I stop, appalled by the sudden enormous void, the abrupt falling away of solid ground.

129

It sucks the air out of my chest. Somehow, however, I know I must get across, and it must happen now. It is not clear what creates this urgency, but the compulsion is real. I must get across.

For a moment, I am overcome by the clear knowledge that if I jump, I will die. I stand at the edge, looking down at the river thousands of feet below, and imagine my body hurtling through the air. Panicked, I look up, out across the mesa on the other side of the gorge. And suddenly, as clearly as I had seen the river below a moment before, I am now seeing the mesa beyond. The mesa is as real as the gorge. And in that moment, I know what I can do.

`There is an absolute difference between knowing what you should do and what you can do. One is an intellectual construct, the other comes from deeper knowledge. In the dream, I recognize the presence of this wisdom that is greater than reason. It is obvious.

Yet my mind is chattering: "It's a sheer drop. Thousands of feet. You can't fly. You'll be smashed on the rocks below if you don't die on the descent. No matter what, you will die. The gorge is too wide. No human being could possibly jump across it. It cannot be done. It defies the laws of gravity. Remember Thelma and Louise in their car. This . . . cannot . . . be done!" Compelling chatter, but not so loud as to be deafening, not so loud as to drown out the sound of other words.

The other words, the surer words, say: "Look to the mesa. See yourself running on the mesa on the other side. To start, you will need to run and leap. At the end of the leap, begin running before your feet even touch the other side. Just keep running."

Now I back up a few hundred feet, turn and run full out toward the gorge and leap. What I remember especially is that I am not afraid, but instead feel calm and strong.

I woke up from the dream knowing I had made it to the other side and was continuing my run across the mesa. I woke with a new, tangible understanding of how seemingly unbreachable obstacles can be met. In fact, this is the only way they can be met. My heart sang.

In the last few weeks, I've remembered this dream several times. For months now, I have been exploring the terrain of my new world, a world that began to redefine itself after my ALS diagnosis. I knew that there was a part of this new world that I wanted to avoid, just as on the mesa of my dream. But inexorably, exploration led me closer and closer to that place. It was unavoidable.

Life is an adventure. When we stop seeing it as such, we die even as our bodies continue to live. I am now at the edge of the mesa. If I want to continue the adventure—and I do—I must leap. It is too facile to say that I am afraid of death, or afraid of the presumed nature of my death, and that I must, therefore, confront and overcome my fear. More, I must understand my fear, and through that understanding gain compassion for myself. It is this compassion, this love, that will carry me across safely.

Everywhere I turn, my life is filled with grace. I can ask for help and expect to receive it. I need help getting across the gorge, need to feel again that calm strength that lets me know that the thing I am about to do, which feels so fraught with mortal danger, will end safely.

What the dream has taught me is that I have to imagine myself fully and completely on the other side. I have to animate this image with as much clarity and specificity as I can. I know what the terrain on this side of the gorge looks like. Now I need to describe the mesa on the other side. I don't need to worry about how I will get there. I only need to think about what it will be like when I am there.

I'm not talking about a quick fix here. Nor am I talking about a transitory state. I'm talking about moving into this "house" full-time and forever. In this state, death is not fearful but just another adventure—albeit, a big adventure. This state cannot be diminished by illness, even an illness that leaves one completely helpless and dependent, one in which, in the end, one cannot even communicate one's wishes, even as the mind remains fully aware. People who live in this house live always and only in the present moment. For them, the past and the future are of no consequence. They live in the present and the present is always perfect.

I left out a very important part of my dream. It happened in two stages. As I stood on the side of the gorge preparing to leap, I saw someone running on the mesa on the other side. At first, I saw someone, anyone. And then I asked the question: "What would it look like if that someone were me?" At that moment, my own body merged with the generic body, and I felt myself running.

Now I ask myself again "What would it look like if that someone were me?"

Part Three

21 February 2006

Dear Ones,

So much time has passed since I last checked in. Time enough for Scott to arrive home safely from Iraq, time enough to get through the holidays, and time enough to complete a trip down to North Carolina to see my sister and celebrate the birthday of her rambunctious, cantankerous three-year old. Time enough also to make me question: Why has it taken me so long to write to you?

The simple answer is that, especially since the first of the year, I have had a curiously difficult time accomplishing much of anything. I've explained my resolve to remain steadfastly myself and not become a disease. However, in its insidious little way, the disease caught up and overtook me, without my being aware of it. These last few months, I've been like a runner in a race on a beautiful day becoming so intoxicated by my surroundings that I didn't notice the other runners passing me by.

Breathing is so important, don't you think? In fact, most of us don't think about our breathing unless we're reminded. I know I didn't until Dr. Joshi got me doing *pranayama* (breathing exercises) everyday. Even then, though I noticed subtle changes in my breathing, I didn't really pay attention. For example, last spring I was having a leisurely lunch with two friends—a little sushi, a lot of talking—when suddenly, in the middle of telling a story, I noticed that I needed to catch my breath. Such a small thing. I noticed it, but that was all.

It happened again when I was talking. Then I noticed that sometimes during the night I would wake up needing to catch my breath. Each time, a simple deep inhalation would get me going again. I was the runner focused on the beautiful day, unaware of the intermittent moments that required conscious deep breathing. At the same time, I was oblivious of something else. Ever so subtly, my breathing was becoming shallower. It happened so incrementally that I was entirely unaware of it. However, I remarked on something else to my doctor when I saw her for my annual physical last October. I noticed that I was tired all the time. I had no stamina. At first it seemed the fatigue was confined to my legs, but as time went on, I realized my entire body was just plain pooped.

By the time Scott got home in January, my days had become pretty circumscribed. Getting up in the morning, putting on clothes, and making meals for myself consumed my day. Taking a shower was a major event. Anyone listening to me complain about how long it took me to take a shower might have wondered if something was amiss. But I am stubborn and obtuse. It wasn't until a regularly scheduled appointment with my neurologists last week that all the pieces came together.

The simple fact is that my diaphragm has not been working properly for some time. Hence, carbon dioxide has been building up in my body, probably for months. The result: fatigue, headaches, neck pain, stomachache, muscle weakness and general malaise. It's amazing how something so profound can sneak up on you unawares. Of course, I also have to give some credit to whatever level of denial I am still harboring.

So, I have crossed over a threshold: I can no longer breathe effectively on my own and have been given a machine called a BiPAP, which stands for "bi-level positive airway pressure." I plug into it for a few hours every day, and it allows me to breathe deeply and completely. I started using it five days ago, and am definitely feeling better.

So I've crossed another threshold: I need help breathing, and from here on out, I will always need help breathing. A little piece of my ship of denial has broken off and is floating away. In retrospect, it's a good thing that Dr. Joshi is so insightful; it should be obvious to anyone that my going to India this year would have been extremely ill-advised.

Every three months, I make a trip to Mass General to see my neurologists. They are all wonderful, caring and delightful people. Given the limitations of the medicine and culture within which they practice, they take excellent care of me. Nonetheless, the days that follow these appointments are always low points. It's like someone giving you a well-intentioned punch in the stomach. It takes your breath away and leaves you reeling for a while. But this last appointment left us all genuinely grieving, largely because my breath capacity has become so compromised.

Yet even in this grieving lies great strength and power. Grieving is like a trap door into the heart. You drop down suddenly and fall straight to the depths. But what is waiting in the depths is not darkness. The other night, Scott, Galen, and I had a conversation about what we want for ourselves and each other: It was pure truth. The answer came straight from the heart to the heart, no side trips. Pearls fell from our mouths. We spoke about the true nature of love.

I know I've been out of touch for too long. I wish I could say that I've been so distracted by life in all its glory that I sometimes just don't have time to write. But life has been a little too damn serious lately. Let the fun and frivolity resume!

My deep love to all of you,
Catherine

21 March 2006

Dear Ones,

For my 50th birthday in 1998, my family decided we should all become certified scuba divers. It was an inspired gift, to say the least. In our imaginations, we saw ourselves gliding through warm tropical waters, consorting with exotic, brightly colored fish along some coral reef. In the short term however, we found ourselves consorting with other neophyte divers in a swimming pool at a high school in Quincy.

After several sessions of classroom study and gamboling in the water to acquaint ourselves with the vagaries of wetsuits, oxygen tanks, flotation vests, flippers, goggles and the like, the big day finally came. In waist deep water, we were instructed to put our regulators (breathing tubes) in our mouths, squat down underwater, and take a deep breath. Until you have been told to put your head under water and inhale, you have no idea how uncompromised your survival instincts truly are. As I looked around me in the pool, I saw people doing exactly what I was doing—trying to convince ourselves that, despite a lifetime of evidence to the contrary, taking a deep breath while submerged was a *good* idea. I don't know if anyone held his or her breath longer than I did, but in the end, I managed a tentative gulp of air, followed by a long, deep, luxurious breath, followed by a fit of giggles. It was glorious.

My experience the first time I used my BiPAP was similar to scuba diving. To be sure, I did not have visions of tropical waters dancing in my head. Better, I had visions of some semblance of a normal life restored. Indeed, that has been the outcome. I plug myself into the machine three times a day for about an hour each time, and at the end of each session, I feel renewed energy. Quite literally, I can breathe again. I recently read an article by a woman who has had ALS since 1985. She was extolling the advances in technology during that time. One of her favorites is the invention of the BiPAP. I can see why. Until I started to have trouble breathing, my favorite new tool had been my voice recognition software. But breathing is breathing. Nothing can beat it.

Scott says I actually look oddly aquatic when I'm using the machine. But lately I have pictured myself differently. I am more like a space alien. On my planet, gravity has less pull and we breathe something other than oxygen. So to be able to manage on Earth, I need support. That's why I need the cane and the wheelchair. That's why I need a breathing machine. This means, of course, that I am here under an alias. My real name is Queen Oola of Zörg. (My sister Amanda in Iowa got the name just right!)

And then there is simply the sense that I am being deconstructed. Is it the deconstruction of some magnificent stone edifice, taken down and carefully numbered for reconstruction on some other site? Not really. It is more like the gentle wearing away that happens over time to movie sets of western towns carefully constructed in the desert. The movie is finished. The crew moves on. Nature takes its course. And eventually, all that is left is what was there before: sand and sagebrush. I am not at all troubled by this image. In my mind, it speaks to two things: the truth about the impermanence of everything physical and the truth about what is actually permanent—not the things we build, but the things we leave behind when the structures are gone.

As we used to say in the 60s, "*Heavy, man.*" But to continue this thought one step further, I am reminded of a dream I had while in India. It was one of those dreams that leaves an emotional charge.

In the dream, I am in a dark room. At one end of the room there is a warm glow. Drawing nearer, I discover that the source of the brightness is candles on a low altar. The altar has on it images of assorted dieties, central among them my own beloved meditation master. I am drawn to this altar with a longing so intense that I begin to cry. I kneel before the altar, weeping, and then am suddenly aware that the altar is leaning against a wall. Looking up. my eye travels along the wall to a window. Standing there, framed by the window, is my meditation master.

She signals me to join her. I walk over and boldly lean my elbow on the windowsill. The height of the window places me slightly below her. She sees that I have been crying, and says two things to me:

"Don't worry. Everyone here loves you."

She pauses for a moment, and then continues:

"You can't stay here."

I look away from her, thinking about what she has said. When I look back, she is gone. I want to see where she has gone, but the window is too high for me to put my head through. Looking for a door, I discover the wall is actually a stage set. A few feet from the edge of the window, the wall ends abruptly. Quickly, I run around to the other side. There she is, walking away, surrounded by a group of children. I call her, and she stops. I run up to her and ask her to embrace me. Immediately, as if we are sisters, she hugs me and then continues her walk with the children.

For several days after this dream, I could not recall the second thing she said to me: "You can't stay here." It was too painful at first to carry those words into my waking life. But eventually, the message came back to me and left me wondering what it could mean. I'm a rather literal thinker, so I figured she meant that I either needed to find a new meditation master or she was stating the obvious: I am dying. No wonder I didn't want to remember her words!

But somehow this interpretation did not feel complete, so I started relating this dream to anyone who would listen. I'm sure it got a little boring to be on the receiving end, but because I'd had the dream in the middle of *panchakarma,* (process of internal cleansing) I felt sure there must be more to it. Finally, my friend Mary unraveled it for me.

Some time ago, I wrote that my goal is to find myself in the state of the "eternal present," a state of bliss that many religious and spiritual traditions describe as enlightenment or liberation. Like most of us, I imagine this condition to be difficult to attain. But in this dream, I was being shown that the separation between where I am now and where I would like to be is nothing more substantial than a fake wall. Furthermore, I was being told that my progress from one state to the other is real and unconditional. It is a fact. The dream seemed to describe not only my situation, but the human condition.

I don't dream a lot, and when I do, I often forget my dreams. This one, however, for obvious reasons, continues to capture my imagination. It has taken me a year to write about this dream—

that's how long it has been percolating. Like the BiPAP, this dream represents a threshold into a new way of life, a new way of thinking, a new way of going about my day, and an indication of what lies ahead.

Recently, my friend Eleanor remarked: "Here's what your updates mean to me. You are going somewhere, and dammit, the rest of us are going with you. If we don't like it, we can stop reading any time."

A week or so ago, a wise person suggested to me that I should find a way to have a party, to gather together all the people I love to let them know how much they mean to me, and to be reminded of their love for me. Chronic illness can be very isolating. I'm not much of a party girl, so I wasn't sure, at first, what to do with this advice. And then I realized that these updates are my party, and that you all are my beloved guests. Thank you for coming.

All my love,
Catherine

19 April 2006

Dear Ones,

When both your parents were raised by Southern mothers, you understand very early that the road to hell is not paved with good intentions, but with unwritten thank you notes. One of my earliest Christmas presents was a box of thank you note cards. I love receiving your notes telling me you are grateful for being invited to my "party." Of course, I am ecstatic to know that you are there. So thank you . . . for your thank you.

The house saga now seems to have come to a resolution. About a month ago, our realtor cautioned us that, given the current real estate market, we should not expect to sell our house this spring. There is simply too much inventory. If we are absolutely determined to sell, we must be willing to drop our price by at least $100,000. Our housing alternatives—whether to build or to buy locally—do not have that kind of financial flexibility. In fact, the only place in our housing scenario with any flexibility at all seems to be the first floor of 1 Larchmont Street. So we have determined to stay put and make some necessary adjustments to the house we are in. Though it's not the simplest solution, at this point it feels right.

To that end, we have consulted with an architect who has given us good advice. We will expand the downstairs bathroom, which may actually entail building out the back of the house a couple of feet. We'll also need to pave the back yard and install a wheelchair lift. Already, we have moved my office down into the front room. Soon, the dining room will be converted into a bedroom. Because stairs are dangerous and energy taxing, these transformations cannot come soon enough, as far as I am concerned.

My dance with the BiPAP continues. I was warned that it would take some time to become truly comfortable with it. How right they were! After using it faithfully for seven weeks, my headaches, sleeplessness and fatigue returned. Discouraged, I called my nurse practitioner, who was appalled to learn my respiratory therapist had not been to see me since she dropped off the machine, a miscommunication that was immediately remedied. She reset the machine to produce a higher volume of air, taught me how to reset it myself, and we (my dance partner and I) seem to be doing better. I still must use the BiPAP during the day because I find it too uncomfortable to wear at night.

So that's the practical side of my life this month. Now on to broader, more philosophical subjects: we're going to talk about God and about death. Too heavy? Skip to the end.

I agree with the Dali Lama that God is compassionate, not vengeful in any way. If God is compassionate, then life's big events are acts of BIG compassion, not exceptions to the rule. So within this context, here is how I understand this stage of my life. Here, in fact, is how I understand ALS.

ALS is an invitation to a conscious death. I can choose to accept the invitation or decline it. This choice is not like a fork in the woods, where choosing one direction means forsaking the other. This choice is more like sailing into the wind. Some days I tack in one direction and some days in the other. On most days, however, I lean toward acceptance.

But I must ask a practical question: Why have I been given so many years to watch myself die? There are no mistakes. There are no coincidences. Life is exact. I must think about how I will die and how I will live. No one does this on a whim. Our culture is not comfortable with the subject. If I were not a daily witness to my obvious loss of physical vitality, I would not be comfortable with it either!

Some days I fall too easily into a kind of stasis; my energy level and ambition are low. I become aware that I am waiting—waiting to die. Since, by all accounts, this is not going to happen soon, I try to catch myself and edge back into the flow of life. But I am aware that life is going on without me simply because I can no longer physically participate.

The prevailing logic is that I am a hapless victim. While I reject this image out of hand, I still ponder the assumption that I am somehow less fortunate than others. Yes, I am different, physically, and to a certain extent mentally, every day. But I think I have been too willing to conclude that this change is bad. I will acknowledge that change is often difficult. I must be careful, however, not to equate change with misfortune.

To what extent is my current unhappiness—and there is a fair amount of that—the result of conditioning? Am I unhappy because

I have not been given what I want or had expected from life? Is that what my culture has taught me? Now, more than ever, I must have a mind of my own, not the culture's. I must interpret my situation in new ways. Just because I am told something is bad does not make it so.

Brave words. Brave thoughts. At the timely suggestion of a friend, I have just finished reading Sherwin Nuland's *How We Die.* The book is slightly dated, but beautifully describes what happens to the physical body when it dies. It is in no way morbid or depressing. To the contrary, it is extraordinarily life-affirming. Death is change. It is neither bad nor good. It is simply a fact.

Every day I am graphically watching myself die. This is a fact, neither good nor bad. You have all been issued an invitation to my party. I will do my best to be a good host. In return, there is something you can do for me. I have trouble consistently remembering that my life still has choices. Primarily, I have trouble remembering that life is not unremittingly sad. I need your help to remind me of the joy and the laughter. I seem to have at present, an unerring faculty for gravitating toward the lugubrious. Help me catch myself. Help me keep things light. Perhaps by doing so you will serve us both.

A couple of months ago, I realized I needed to do something to counteract what I saw as a growing tendency toward passivity—the sense that I was simply waiting to die. So, I signed up for a writing course at U Mass Boston! Well, right away I got something that made me feel young and vital again—a University of Massachusetts student ID. Never mind that the dreadful picture on the ID makes me look older than Methuselah—I am a student again! The man who teaches the course is wonderful—encouraging, funny, knowledgeable, and trustworthy. We have to write something every week. Each week, as Wednesday approaches, I have to get something, anything, on paper. Below is the first piece I wrote for the course. Think of it as the dessert part of our party.

All my love,
Catherine

Carry the One
The Remains

On a winter evening of my junior year in college, my ancient and venerable VW bug and I are halfway home for Christmas vacation, when I realize it needs gas. It has been several years since the gas gauge actually worked, so my mind has to keep a perpetual tally. In the snowy darkness, I look for a place to pull in.

I am anxious to get home. I have stayed at school a few days longer to finish up some work. I won't be back until fall. Everything I own is packed in the VW. In another week, I will be in Paris. I could have waited out the storm and gone home the next day, but I am thinking about Paris. I am excited and anxious and can no longer tolerate the confines of my little dorm room. So here I am on a stormy winter night pulling off the highway.

On the exit ramp, I notice the snow is mixed with rain. The windshield is matted with soggy clumps of snow. The road gleams, black and blinding, with the headlights from other cars. I see the bright lights of the gas station and pull in.

It's a Volkswagen, so the gas tank is in the front, under the hood. No wonder I always wait until the last minute to refill it. First, the hood must be unlocked by pulling a steel rod inside the car. On a frigid night, that's the easy part. Then, standing outside in front of the car, I must raise the icy hood, revealing the gas cap. Everything is metal.

This lengthy production finished, I am finally back behind the wheel, chilled to the bone and grateful for a robust heating system. I roll out of the gas station and onto the access road. Up ahead, I see a line of cars poised to precede me back to the highway. I apply the brakes. Nothing happens. I brake again. Still nothing. I swerve to avoid hitting the car ahead of me. I almost clear it.

I hear the impact, the dull thud of metal on metal. My head hits the steering wheel. In my hurry to get back on the road, I have neglected to put on my seat belt. I look up and see the world in a blur—my glasses are gone. But the gold haze before my eyes is unmistakable: Flames are shooting up from the front of the car. My mind forms only one thought: "Get out!"

I reach for the door handle and lean into the door. No response. The door is stuck. I feel the first prick of panic. Leveraging myself between the steering wheel and the back of the seat, I swivel, bring my knees to my chest, and kick out the door. Suddenly the car and I are both in motion. My feet hit the pavement and go out from under me on the black ice. The car, like a flaming comet, slowly and gently glides across the road into a nearby field. There it sits, quietly burning. By the time the fire engines arrive, the car and everything in it are black ashes and twisted metal.

Oblivious to the danger of standing in the middle of a road, in the middle of a storm, in the middle of the night, I watch the car's serene trajectory. I see the blackness of the night and then, all around me, small white spheres bouncing on the road. Others stop to watch, too. A woman scoops up a handful of the spheres and brings them to me.

"I saved as many of them as I could."

Looking at her offering, I almost laugh, "Thanks, but don't bother. They're not real."

For the rest of the night, as I am interviewed by the police, as I am taken to the hospital in shock, with badly bruised knees and a concussion, I hold the tiny balls in my hand. They are all that is left. Five fake pearls.

29 May 2006

Dear Ones,

Whenever I hear about people wanting to "balance their lives," I imagine someone standing with one leg on a block of ice and the other in a blazing fire, trying to feel pleasantly warm. Like most people, I tend to hop up and down, first on one leg and then on the other, trying to avoid the severe consequences of standing too long in one place.

On the practical front, our friend Paul, who has been staying with us for the past few months, has been the ideal person to help us resolve the accessibility issues in our house. We had consulted an architect about making some fairly significant changes to the first floor—a larger bathroom and a reconfigured backyard and garage with wheelchair lift to the deck. This was all going to be mind-bogglingly expensive, and it led to a moment of real clarity.

If I were going to be living in this house for many years, important and expensive renovations would make sense. However, our solutions do not have to be elegant. After all, they will only be used for a short time. Enter Paul. By profession, he is a master carpenter, set designer and builder—supremely gifted in the art of the serviceable, short-term solution. He has already devised an answer to the current shortcomings of the downstairs bathroom and is now working on the exterior access issues. He and Scott have just installed a wheelchair lift (thank you Craig's list!) onto the front porch. Reconfiguration of a portion of the same front porch will follow.

As of last week, my whole operation has moved to the first floor. What had once been our family room is now my bedroom. What had once been our front room and meditation room is now my office. Soon the massage table will also find itself on the first floor. The house is looking decidedly strange. It's like a giant hourglass with furniture for sand. Over the weeks, the furniture has been slowly settling at the bottom of the house, leaving the upstairs looking barren, and the downstairs looking like a tag sale.

One more practical, "outer world" item before shifting to the inner world. Scott received word at the end of last week that he will return to Iraq in early June. This time, he'll be gone for about a month. This fact coincides with another: I now need daily assistance. My right hand has become considerably weaker. My left hand is virtually useless. My legs support me only briefly. The time has come to get some help. Like many others in our situation, our health insurance does not cover a home health aide. So we are investigating creative solutions. Once again, our house is proving to be an invaluable asset: We have lots of room. If you happen to know an unfailingly cheerful individual who would like to trade room and board for 15 or so hours of help a week, please let us know and we will give you more details.

Yes, Scott is really going back to Iraq. Although I am physically weaker than when he last went, in some ways I'm in better shape.

I know what to expect now. I no longer have to climb stairs. And it's summer. Everything seems easier in warm weather, don't you think?

Moving on to the inner world. Here, things have become decidedly esoteric. I've been thinking and experiencing things that seem so otherworldly as to be almost indescribable. They border on what my siblings would refer to as "ugga-bugga"—bizarre, and even a little mysterious. As I often say, welcome to my world! Some of this stuff is very hard to describe, especially one experience, several weeks ago.

For the past few years I have had the extraordinary good fortune to be under the care of a cranio-sacral therapist named Nicole. During my sessions with her I lie on a well-padded massage table and, through a simple laying on of hands, she guides me to a place of deep stillness. Of all the things I'm doing to support myself, this practice is the most valuable.

A recent session with Nicole began with a sensation of warmth deep in my belly. It was similar to the feeling one gets from leg muscles after a warm-up: a sudden surge of energy and power. The energy began low in my pelvis and grew quickly. When it reached the size of a basketball, it began to move.

In less than a second, it moved to my chest and then shot down to the soles of my feet. Just as quickly, it rolled back up the full length of my body and exited through the top of my head. It was substantial— solid yet soft—and moved with calm, purposeful authority. Speed was its very nature.

Like an outside observer, I saw my body in two places at once. I saw my physical body as a container, like a suitcase. But I was aware of something else far greater that was also me: my true self, powerful and immortal. The same body: one compromised, the other invincible.

Through the eyes of my greater self, I saw my physical body and had compassion for its frailty. I recognized how afraid I have been— afraid of loss, of helplessness, of the future, of sadness, of anger, of despair, and of tears. I was overcome with love for this delicate, troubled and humbled being.

After the ball of energy had completed its course, I opened my eyes. For a moment, I lay on the table absolutely still. All around me was absolute stillness. Slowly, I sat up and lowered my feet to the floor, which felt cool and firm. I felt strength flowing through my legs. I sat down in a chair and again felt my feet solidly on the floor. My rear end, the backs of my thighs and my shoulder blades firmly met the chair. My forearms were tingling. My breath was slow, deep, and relaxed. Ecstasy bubbled up and I began to cry and laugh.

Overwhelmed by gratitude, a prayer formed on my lips. I asked to remain in this state for the rest of my life, or at least to retain the full imprint of the experience. Even before the request was spoken, I knew it had been granted.

Nicole said quietly, "You're on the other side of the gorge." She was referring to my dream from several months ago about the Rio Grande Gorge.

I asked, with awe and excitement, of no one in particular, "What happens next?"

What happened in the next few weeks was anger: incisive, sudden, and indiscriminate. I can no more control it than I can control a hiccup. I have felt lost, as though I have slipped my moorings and am adrift in an uncharted sea. Why anger? Why this lashing out? It seems an expression of fear, stemming from a gnawing anxiety, like going into a final exam I'd forgotten to study for.

After Nicole welcomed me to the other side of the gorge, I saw myself doing a gleeful victory dance, my arms raised in the air, my feet bounding. At the same time, however, I had a sense that I had left something back on the other side. "Good riddance!" I thought. Whatever I had left behind was unworthy, even hateful. Where I was going, I neither needed nor wanted its company. If it did not have the wherewithal to leap the gorge with me, it could not presume to come on the rest of my journey. Such vehemence! Such righteousness! Such anger!

Such blindness. This is not how life works. One does not progress by throwing aside and abandoning psychic body parts. So I took myself back to the edge of the gorge. I looked across, back from where I had come. On the other side was a small dark figure. It was calling out to me, its arms outstretched, its cries plaintive. In that moment, I knew I would have to go back.

When I returned to the gorge, it had become smaller. No longer an insurmountable chasm, it had become a small crack in the earth. I had become a colossus, while the figure on the other side was very small. With a foot on each side of the gorge, I nimbly reached down and scooped up the small figure with my right arm. I perched it on my hip like a baby and snuggled it against my body. Instantly, it melted into me. I turned and continued on my journey, the gorge at my back.

I have no doubt the gorge is at my back. I also have no doubt that other gorges, in other forms, lie ahead.

All my love,
Catherine

30 June 2006

Dear Ones,

Scott left for Iraq again last Wednesday. I'm not sure what astrological forces were at work during the 24 hours before his departure, but by the time he left, I felt as though a powerful wind had descended upon us and blown us both to separate worlds. In the week that followed, both of us were so consumed by the flow of events in our individual lives that neither of us had the time or the energy to think much about each other. I expected this would be the case for him, but not for me.

The day before he left was the setup. That afternoon as he was running the washing machine, sudsy water began to back up into the laundry room. A bad sign, though I can't say we were surprised. Full disclosure: We have been aware for the past four years that trouble was brewing in our sewer line. Timing in life truly is everything, and this timing was exquisite. Here was Scott on the eve of departure for Iraq. There was, beyond a doubt, nothing he could do. So that left . . . moi.

Under the best of circumstances, I would find dealing with a sewer problem a little stressful. But these days, as I feel increasingly more helpless, the dread was palpable. I prayed for a quick, cheap fix and called the plumber. He came, and the answers to the prayer were "no" and "no." It was expensive and would take an entire week. I no longer need to worry about getting the lawn mowed while Scott's away. No more lawn. The hole was deep and wide. Ultimately, the sewer was fixed. It's amazing what one will put up with for the privilege of flushing the toilet and taking a shower.

Before you begin to feel too sorry for me, I should hasten to add that I had tremendous support throughout all of this. As Scott was getting ready to leave, my friend Sarah stepped in as she did during his last trip to Iraq. Sarah, Diane, and Jean—wonderful neighbors for many years—set up a network of volunteer support: meals, grocery shopping, errands, drivers, and people to help me into and out of bed every day. She also discovered a singular web site designed to coordinate volunteers who want to help someone in need. Check it out: www.lotsahelpinghands.com. The web site covers my daily needs and it also brought help during the sewer crisis.

A high point this month was a visit with Dr. Joshi on his last day in Boston. I was able to spend a couple of hours with him. Of course, he asked all sorts of probing questions about my digestive performance. To my credit, I no longer blush or stammer as I give him the unabridged details. Thanks to his herbs, my digestive track is stunningly efficient. But this is not the thing that he found remarkable. After he had listened to my pulses and asked his questions, he pushed back his chair and looked me in the eye.

"I must tell you that I'm confused. You are teaching me. I see with my eyes and understand you in one way. I listen to your pulses and measure your *doshas*, and I understand you completely differently."

I listened to this introduction with growing apprehension. I have been fearful for some time that before too long Dr. Joshi will tell me there is nothing more he can do. He continued to speak.

"When I saw you walking up the path today, I saw that you are significantly weaker than the last time I saw you. I was sure that when I measured your *doshas*, they would be all over the place. Instead, they are exactly as they were the last time I saw you. In fact, they have changed very little over the time I have known you. This tells me that some part of you is still actively fighting this illness."

Then he gave a little chuckle, shrugged his shoulders and said, "You are Durga. What can I say? You are a warrior." (Durga is the great Hindu warrior goddess. Her name in Sanskrit translates as "invincible." She usually appears seated on a lion.)

Dr. Joshi went on to assure me that as long as my doshas are stable, he wants to treat me. So he prescribed a new round of unpleasant and nasty tasting herbs—except for the large yellow pills that he says are for "sadness" and look like they should have happy faces on them. He encouraged me to stay on his diet as much as I could, and continue pranayama and yoga to the best of my ability. I told him that I no longer do my own cooking, so I have to believe that the food I receive, which is prepared with such loving care, will have to do. Hearing this, he insisted that, at least for that night, I would eat properly because he would feed me. We then went into the house and I watched him make chapatis to go with the rice and simple beans and vegetables he had prepared earlier. We ate well, and mostly in silence. Leaving, I felt, as always, that I had been blessed by a unique and powerful healer.

This high point was followed closely by another. As you know, I have been trying to find a particular kind of bed, a non-hospital bed with adjustable head and foot. Scott and I went on a reconnaissance mission to a local furniture store. Wow, they are expensive! So we looked for a used one on Craig's list, but in the weeks that followed saw nary a one. However, shortly after our visit to the furniture store, I received an envelope in the mail. Inside was a check from a friend of a friend—someone I have met only once. It was large enough to allow me to buy the new bed!

Even as I write this, I am still stunned by this act of grace and generosity from someone who hardly knows me. The bed is a double blessing. On a practical level, it is something I need and already use constantly. On another level, it reminds me that I don't need to worry. It confirms once again that all will be well. For all of this, I am once again humbled by gratitude.

Of less importance this month, I have endured a sleep study, a contradiction in terms if ever I heard one. It was a complete bust and will have to be repeated. Its purpose was to determine what kind of breathing support, especially at night, would best serve me. As I become more and more involved with the American medical system, I am learning how very often the simplest things can go awry. In the meantime, the BiPAP and I have reached an accommodation. If I ever expected more than this, perhaps I was being too optimistic. It is keeping my carbon dioxide levels under control but when I'm using it, I still swallow lots of air. This latter condition makes me particularly wonderful company. One way or another, air is constantly passing through my body. 'Nuff said. I'm beginning to see a pattern that you've no doubt already discerned. Ayurveda? Sewer lines? BiPAP air? Oh Lord, my life is becoming one big potty joke.

These days, I tend to use a walker around the house; excursions outside the house are done in a wheelchair. I no longer drive. The increasing weakness in my right hand, along with the complete loss of my left hand, makes even the simplest tasks long, arduous, and often unsuccessful. Someone must always be with me overnight. So, I need help all the time, and help means people. I am fortunate to be surrounded by loving, cheerful, and understanding friends and family. It's not as if there's an ogre standing at the foot of my bed in the morning, helping me start my day. It's always someone I love. What could be better than that? And yet, it's taking some time to adjust. I still treasure my solitude, necessarily limited though it is.

Finally, I want to share the after effects of the experience I described in my last update. Intellectually, I seem to be in complete denial that it ever happened. However, I have been aware since then of a very strange physical phenomenon: I feel as though my skin has become very thin, as if I am insubstantial, almost incorporeal. For someone who has always felt robust and solid, this is a very odd feeling, yet one that doesn't seem to have any emotion attached to it at all. Everything just feels soft and thin. Do with that as you may. I haven't a clue.

All my love,
Catherine

8 August 2006

Dear Ones,

Scott has returned home from Iraq. Now we are playing catch-up. First and foremost, we had to catch up with his 60th birthday, which we did last night, 2+ weeks after-the-fact. On his first day home, however, Scott took one look at the sewer-crisis sinkhole adorning our yard and rolled his eyes. Fortunately, the debilitating heat and humidity of the previous weeks has abated, so the weather for yard work is much finer. The irony of Scott's work in Iraq is that it is always somewhat sedentary. They are out in the weather all day (this time in temperatures of 118° upwards), but they are minding machinery. And when they are not minding machinery, they are waiting for transportation. It's a test of patience and physical and mental endurance more than physical strength. So, moving some earth in the yard will give him some much-needed exercise.

It turns out that I, while Scott was gone, had been holding my breath, literally and figuratively. I didn't realize to what degree until he had been home for about 24 hours. Despite my absolute need for all of the loving care I received from so many in Scott's absence,

I still persisted in imagining myself as largely independent. What folly is this? It's just that I have always reveled in my ability to take care of myself and in my joy at my own company. So, despite all appearances to the contrary, I have continued to believe that this is still my prevailing state. You all who take such extraordinary care of me know how deluded I am. In all honesty, and many of you may be relieved to hear me own up to this, I know that I could not now survive without you. And you have been compassionate to the extreme. You have allowed me to come to the end of my illusion on my own.

The morning after Scott returned home, he embraced me and I let out an enormous, tearful sigh and then was laid low by a 24-hour mystery malady. Despite this, the fact is that when Scott got home, I finally felt safe. It's not that, during his absence, I was aware of feeling unsafe. Quite to the contrary, I was surrounded by people who made it clear to me they would and could do anything for me. Intellectually, I could not imagine being less vulnerable, and yet at a deeper level, I felt more so. In a way, it's like being taken care of by an entire practice of ideal doctors who are all skilled, intuitive, compassionate, and care for me deeply, but because of their numbers, cannot give me continuity of care. Despite their best intentions, there are just too many of them, and I have to manage the interactions among them.

I am not complaining. Please rest assured, I am not complaining. In most respects, I had an absolutely wonderful time while Scott was gone. I had the unique experience of spending uninterrupted, blissful (what we used to call "quality") time with the women I love most in the world. In fact, I came away with many happy memories—Cathy taking on and meticulously conquering a number of the operational anomalies that had been limiting my independence; Darnella (henceforth to be known as Deadeye) dispatching mosquitoes by night and gourmet food and foot massages by day; Galen of the magic hands expertly curing a migraine; Amanda making me laugh; splendid meals with Becket (and more laughter); and Paula and Inara sitting at the foot of my bed each massaging one of my feet and telling stories. And then there was Jean's garden party, going to the movies with Diane, and the sure and comforting knowledge that Sarah was never far away. It was a full time. I would not have missed it for the world.

But, note to self: "Listen old darlin'," (as my grandmother used to say), "you can't go on like this."

I know the time has come to have a consistent person take care of me. I need one "doctor" now, and that doctor cannot be Scott. It needs to be someone whose purpose for being in my house is to be there for me. I mentioned this to Becket before she left. She surprised and delighted me by saying, "That's fine. But when Scott goes away again, I still want to come and be with you." I like the idea that it's not an either/or proposition. I can have both. Ain't I the lucky one?

Embedded in that last paragraph, sharp eyes will have noted the phrase "when Scott goes away again." Yes, folks, it's bound to happen again. Another trip to Iraq is a distinct possibility. And even without that, as I have said before, this is how Scott makes his living. He must be able to travel. At least for the time being, this necessity and my needs are not incompatible. It's just going to take some effort and some grace to find the right solution/person. A number of you offered a variety of options we might pursue in locating such a person, a caring, cheerful someone, who would be interested in bartering room and board for 15 hours a week of my care. At that time, though,

Scott had just left for Iraq, and I did not feel comfortable embarking on this by myself. Now that he's home, the time is ripe.

And what about the BiPAP? I know you have been bearing with me thus far just to get to the latest installment of "As the BiPAP Blows," an ongoing saga in many parts. Early in July, I was able to visit one of my favorite places in the whole world—Cathy's farm in New Hampshire. The second day there turned warm and sultry. By the middle of the night, the air was completely still. I woke up twice, not sure what had awakened me, and went back to sleep. The third time, however, irritated by my inability to settle into sleep again, I became aware of the cause. I was laboring to breathe. The nice thing about the semi-wakeful state is that it tends to be calm. So, with infinite logic and not a trace of panic, I knew the solution lay right beside me. I reached for my BiPAP mask, put it on, and pushed the air button. Thus remedied, I fell into a deep and untroubled sleep. So began my ability to sleep through the night using the BiPAP. I now sleep with it on every night. Tomorrow, I will have my second sleep study—or we might say the first one, given the complete inadequacy of the previous one. That should help me fine tune the good thing I have going now. So stay tuned for another thrill-packed adventure.

My friend Marcia recently sent me a quote, which I unfortunately seem to have mislaid, from someone whose life is similar to my own. Basically, he commented that illness is something his body is going through but it is not who he is. He is who he has always been, undiminished by illness. Of course, you know I completely subscribe to this perspective. I find, in fact, that the more I lose my physical abilities, the more I quite naturally am disconnecting my awareness of my body from my awareness of all else. This goes against my training and life as a dancer, in which I naturally came to understand the world as an extension of my body and its abilities. Over and over, I had the experience that physical strength and health were synonymous with psychological and spiritual well-being. Now of necessity, I am discovering the two are not umbilically attached. This new awareness shakes the foundation of my being. There are days, quite honestly, when I do not know who I am, when I find my life utterly confusing.

I have to consider, though, that most of us in our late 50s are pretty set in our ways. We know who we are. We know our world. We know how we prefer to interact with our world. There are few surprises. To arbitrarily choose change, then, is not typical of the human condition. As I've said before, I liked my life. The interesting thing is, I still like my life, but I have been given something truly rare. On the eve of my 58th birthday, I have been given a new life. It's almost as if I have been taken into the witness protection program: I have a new identity; all bets are off; I have to learn to live all over again. I am being required to do what Madonna does so well—reinvent myself. This is a gift not many are given.

As an example of reinvention, one of the things I learned during Scott's absence was how to be with people. Always in the past, I would maintain a certain distance from even my closest friends. I valued my privacy. Now, my privacy has been invaded. I have had to open my life and my heart to a select and beloved circle of family and friends. If I had been told in advance that this would be necessary, I would have been appalled. Instead, and this has taken some practice, I am discovering a sweetness to life that I had missed before. When I think of the happy memories I listed above, I know beyond a doubt that these opportunities would never have been available to me in my previous incarnation. With this knowledge, I treasure them the more.

So once again, to all of you who are so intimately engaged in my transformation, thank you for your love, patience, compassion, forbearance, and, most of all, for your humor. The party is still in full swing. Thanks for bringing the food.

All my love,
Catherine

3 September 2006

Dear Ones,

Hurricane season is upon us and I've had to start wearing socks again. The guy who makes my leg braces is always appalled to see that I insist on going sockless all summer. Apparently, no socks equals blisters, but not in my case. For me, no socks equals happy toes. I'll do pretty much anything to keep my sweet little toes happy. My toes like Tevas, and right now I am compromising their happiness by slipping socks between the toes and the Tevas. It's raining and cool out there. Hurricane Ernesto. Fortunately, thanks to my friend Janet, I have an outstanding, and growing, collection of stylish socks.

Just now, as I've been sitting here watching the rain, my doctor called with the results of the latest sleep study. Yes, this means she called me on Sunday of Labor Day weekend. Lisa Krivickas is that kind of doc—I like her. Anyway, the upshot of the study is that the BiPAP is doing a good job, but there's a slightly different version of the machine that might mitigate some of the air swallowing I'm experiencing. So we're going to give it a try.

August was a month for dancing with doctors. I saw my neurological team a couple of weeks ago, and there is general concern about the list of things that wake me up at night. We all agreed that an attempt to whittle down the list would be worthwhile. Swallowing air wakes me up. Lying in certain positions helps to eliminate the air swallowing, but lying too long in one position makes my neck and legs ache, and that also wakes me up. The hope is that by eliminating the air, we can also eliminate the ache. I'd be very happy to scratch both those items off my list. For now, this is one soap opera that is not likely to be canceled anytime soon.

Seeing the neurological team always results in appointments with my extended medical family. So last week I met with the adaptive technologies person, the sublime woman who helps me locate all those nifty gadgets that replace weak muscles. As the cold weather sets in, not only will I need more substantial footwear, I will also lose most of the use of my right hand. My left hand is already a goner. But Inspector Gadgets is out there, inventing solutions, some of them quite amusing. Think of managing life's intimate daily routines with no hands. Got that? Who knew I would ever need to know this stuff? But I'm glad it's there. Concurrently, my ever-resourceful brace guy is building me a spiffy new right leg.

While enjoying all this medical attention, I have also been reading Jane Redmont's *When in Doubt, Sing: Prayer in Daily Life*. It's an exhaustive and thoughtful look at the role of prayer and the definitions of prayer in modern times. I knew Jane when she lived in Boston and bought her book when it came out in 1999, but am only now getting around to reading it.

Jane makes an important distinction between curing and healing. I have been using the terms interchangeably, but now, through

Redmont, am understanding them as separate entities. It is clear to me that I will most likely not be cured. However, it is also clear to me that this entire illness has and will continue to be an experience of healing. I'm sure many of you can relate to this from your own experience. It occurs to me that, asked to choose between curing and healing, I would choose the latter. Good choice, yes?

In addition to this perspective on healing, Redmont introduced me to words that have helped me put my life in perspective. In 1981, the revered Jesuit priest Pedro Arrupe suffered a devastating stroke, after which he wrote:

> *More than ever I find myself in the hands of God.*
> *This is what I have wanted all my life from my youth.*
> *But now there is a difference;*
> *The initiative is entirely with God.*
> *It is indeed a profound spiritual experience*
> *To know and feel myself so totally in God's hands.*

I recommend Jane Redmont's book, especially for anyone involved in retreat and spiritual work.

As for curing, there are forces out there hard at work on the curing end of ALS. Anyone who is interested in the details can go to *www.als-mda.org* for all the latest. Anything that is local, I have probably contributed to in some way or another. And for those of you who would like to participate in efforts to find a cure, my splendid nephew, Colin Hale, is providing an opportunity. Colin, in what appears to be a Royce family tradition, temporarily left school and signed on to work at Starbucks. He is putting together a team from his store to participate in the annual Walk to D'Feet ALS on October 14th, in Wakefield, Massachusetts. This will be a district-wide event for Starbucks stores in and around Newton. In addition, daughter Galen has signed on with both her current and former stores in Cambridge and Boston, so this could be big. Friends have promised to push me for the three-mile walk, so I plan on being there and have put in an order for a magnificent fall day. I promise a snazzy pair of socks.

In the meantime, it is likely that Scott will be returning to Iraq on or around September 15th. This time, he'll be gone about a month. I'm getting good at this. My sense of panic is down to a manageable level, and this time I will have even more help. My sister Becket broadcast my quest for a live-in caregiver; after multiple forwardings, the message reached a young woman in Trieste, Italy. We exchanged many e-mails. It turns out that very close family friends of hers live in Newton. She wants to come to this country to improve her English and then, ultimately, go to graduate school here in Boston. Her name is Cristiana, and she will be spending this fall perfecting her English at 1 Larchmont Street and taking care of me. She arrives this coming Thursday!

Finally, as you know, I have been doing a bit of writing beyond these updates. My sisters, my writing class, and especially the incomparable class leader, Carter Jefferson, have become my indispensable editing team. With their support and encouragement, two marvelous things have happened. First of all, a piece of my writing has been published in an online quarterly called Flashquake. (*http://www.flashquake.org/nonfiction*) This particular journal is dedicated to work of 1000 words or less, hence, *flash*. It is a story that describes the first day I ever spent with my oldest friend, Catharine Roehrig—almost 50 years ago.

Secondly, at a friend's suggestion, I have written an essay for the NPR series "This I Believe." I received a very warm personal note from the editor thanking me for my submission. Whether or not it will actually make it onto the air (they have received 15,000 submissions since the project began), the process of discovering that I have a belief and that I can articulate it made the whole exercise worthwhile. I'll let you know if they decide to run it, but, in the interest of sparing your patience, I'm giving you a sneak preview below in "Carry the One." Needless to say, all of this has definitely brightened my day.

All my love,
Catherine

CARRY THE ONE
This I Believe

I believe that I always have a choice. No matter what I'm doing. No matter where I am. No matter what is happening to me. I always have a choice.

Today I am sitting at my computer, speaking these words through a microphone. Although I have spent my life typing on a keyboard, I can no longer use my hands. Every day I sit at my computer speaking words instead of typing. In 2003, I was diagnosed with ALS, Lou Gehrig's Disease. Over time, this disease will weaken and finally destroy every significant muscle in my body. Ultimately, I will be unable to move, to speak, and finally, to breathe. Already, I am largely dependent upon others. So every day I review my choices.

Living with ALS seems a bit like going into the witness protection program. Everything I have ever known about myself—how I look, how I act, how I interact with the world—is rapidly and radically changing. And yet, with each change, I still have choice. When I could no longer type with my hands, I knew I could give up writing entirely or go through the arduous process of learning how to use voice recognition software. I'm not a young woman. This took real work. Interestingly, I write more now than ever before.

At an even more practical level, every day I choose not only how I will live, but if I will live. I have no particular religious mandate that forbids contemplating a shorter life, an action that would deny this disease its ultimate expression. But this is where my belief in choice truly finds its power. I can choose to see ALS as nothing more than a death sentence or I can choose to see it as an invitation—an opportunity to learn who I truly am.

Even people in the witness protection program must take with them fundamental aspects of themselves which can never change. What are these aspects for me? This is what I learn every day, and so far I have discovered many unique things, but one stands out above the rest. I have discovered in myself an ability to recognize, give, and receive caring in a way far deeper than anything in my life previously. Others have seen this in me as well.

I, who have always been an intensely private and independent person, have allowed a wide circle of family and friends into the most intimate parts of my life. Previously, I would have found such a prospect appalling. I might have felt I had no choice but to embrace the assumption that living with ALS means a life of hardship and isolation. Instead, because I believe that I always have a choice, I opened myself to other possibilities. And now the very thing that at first seemed so abhorrent has graced my life with unaccustomed sweetness. It was always there. Only now I have chosen to see it. This sweetness underscores and celebrates my belief that I always have a choice.

1 October 2006

Dear Ones,

When my son Owen was a toddler, he was the king of the temper tantrum. He chose his locations with great care. A particular favorite was a crowded aisle in the grocery store. (For maximum effect, he needed maximum audience.) He would begin by dramatically throwing himself onto the floor, a bloodcurdling "No!" exploding from his lips. He would then scream and flail, arching his back, his little face getting redder and redder. I would calmly step over him, informing him in a quiet voice that I would meet him at the end of the aisle. If he did not have an audience, a cooing grandmotherly type, or perhaps a priest checking to see if the little boy was spewing green vomit, the episode would be brief. At the end of it, he would pick himself up and walk, sniffing as he came, back to my side. I would put him on my hip, give him a quick snuggle, and we would continue on our way. I always felt tremendous compassion for him. He worked so hard.

Well, these days I feel like that: a two-year old. I am the one having the temper tantrums now. And truly, God waits for me at the end of the aisle. My tantrums are all about the things I do not want to do. The basic theme is that I do not want to do my life the way it is currently playing out. I do not want to be tired all the time. I do not want to need help accomplishing the simplest tasks. I do not want to have to breathe through a mask as I try to sleep. I do not want to be cut off from visiting friends because I can no longer get into their houses, or from travel because it is now logistically impossible. I do not want to need an escort every time I leave the house. Simply stated, I do not want to do this. In my last update, I quoted a poem in which I said I felt myself to be "totally in God's hands." Well, I want you to k.now that this is the case but I am not at all happy about it. My temper tantrum, as you can see, has quite a head of steam.

Owen's tantrums were like squalls. They were violent but very temporary upheavals. Mine, however, have been going on for quite a while now and show no sign of blowing out to sea. I have come to visit—and trust it is only a visit—the depths of my own despair. I expect this was always inevitable, but I have to say, it sure isn't any fun. I liken it to pulling a Band-Aid off a very tender wound, slowly. This despair pushes me, as never before, to revisit my intention for my life. That is, to consciously experience my own death.

This is by no means a passive activity. Consciously experiencing my death is very different from passively waiting for it to happen. I feel myself "walking through the valley of the shadow of death" with my eyes wide open. Nothing in my life has prepared me for pain of this magnitude. But the 23rd Psalm is one of my favorites because it doesn't leave you in the valley. It reminds me that we are never alone. Lately, however, I have been feeling very much alone. Not for lack of company—I've had plenty of that. But this dying is a lonely business, and sometimes I need clear and tangible proof that, no matter where I am or what I'm doing, I am never alone.

This is especially true now as I feel myself progressing to the next step. For the last couple of years, I have tended to see myself as someone with a disability. Now, however, as pressure sores, weight-loss, and a persistent cough, among other things, have made their way into my life, my perception has shifted. Now I am more aware of myself as someone who is ill. Of course, I have been ill all along but am only now realizing how nonnegotiable this is. Disability can be managed, but illness . . . it feels somehow more insidious. I need to feel a powerful hand in my hand.

So far, I have been blessed with very particular people to help me walk through this valley. In particular, I have Nicole and Jeff, two people with enormous hearts and deep intelligence who have committed themselves to staying with me wherever I go until I'm gone. I am struck by the fact that since I was diagnosed with ALS, my every need has been immediately and abundantly answered. In every case, I have been given the best. It is a clue that I'm on the right track, that I'm doing what I was sent here to do. I can complain and kick my heels and carry on as much as I want, but none of that behavior in any way alters my purpose.

Another recent magnificent blessing has been the arrival of Cristiana in our house. She is cheerful, smart, funny, absolutely reliable, and willing to do anything I ask. Everything is done with enthusiasm and good humor. She is taking extraordinarily good care of me. I could not have asked for a better companion. She will be here until the end of November, at which time she has to return to Italy. She is applying to graduate school here in Boston and is hoping to begin in January. Her background is child psychology and she wants to get a master's degree in criminal justice so she can work with court-involved youth. We are all beginning to speak with heavy Italian accents here.

Scott leaves for Iraq tomorrow and should be gone about a month. Those of you who signed up on the Helping Hands website in June and July have already received e-mails from the dynamic trio—Sarah, Jean, and Diane—asking once again for your help. As before, the biggest need is for dinners.

"As the BiPAP Blows" has been on hiatus this past month as I wait for the arrival of the new machine. Why it has taken a month to get this machine continues to be a mystery. In the meantime, a truly creative and resourceful person very dear to my heart has come up with a sleep aid. Let's just call it: "special cookies." I eat one at bedtime and, although my sleep is not uninterrupted, I am sleeping more deeply. As an added bonus, I wake up with a raging appetite for breakfast! Works for me. (Someone recently asked me why I don't just eat the cookies all day long. It's a thought, but I'm already enough of a liability using my walker without adding impairment. Also, I don't want to be anesthetized when the sun is shining.)

Special thanks to those of you who have signed on to either participate in or contribute to Colin and Galen's ALS walk on October 14th. They have been joined by a third fundraising angel, Lora Maurer. By the way, for those of you planning on joining us for the walk, I do have, as promised, a new pair of snazzy socks for the occasion. Thank you, Janet!

All my love,
Catherine

25 October 2006

Dear Ones,

My friend Eleanor has been asking me for months now why I am not more angry about this turn my life has taken (after all, she reasons, she's furious about it). For the longest time, I simply didn't feel angry—petulant, yes, but not angry. However, I'm learning that the body and the psyche have their own pace, unique to each of us. I guess I just needed to live with myself, in this state, for a while. I expect also that I might have needed more time than others. I was raised to avoid anger. It was sort of like that admonition our mothers used to tell us when we made a face: "Be careful. Your face might freeze like that." I think I believed anger could do that, too. If I really became angry, I might get stuck there. I've needed time to get past that.

Interestingly, although I can hardly say I have left anger behind (quite to the contrary! I'm going to need to buy a new telephone to replace the one I have pummeled so thoroughly), I have discovered that anger is not exclusive. That is, the mind and body can emotionally multi-task. So, even as I have given myself over to the wonders of anger, I am not angry all the time. I am relieved and delighted to discover this.

This discovery has kept me busy this month (you'll recall my temper tantrums of the last update) and has led the way to a new understanding: I now know the purging properties of white-hot anger. I realized a couple of weeks ago that I finally know, beyond a doubt, that I am not getting my old life back, ever. Somewhere, in the deep recesses of my mind, I seem to have been holding out hope that one morning I would wake up and discover that I was healthy again, and that all of this had just been one of God's little lessons. Lesson learned, I would have my life back. I don't know why I thought this. I don't know how I was able to hold onto this thought for so long. But now it is gone. It's like when they cut down a tree in the forest. At first, you just notice you can see farther, and you're not sure why. Then, when you get closer, you can see the stump and understand what is missing.

A number of people have asked me how I spend my days. (a) Do I spend the day reading? (b) Do I spend the day in meditation? (c) After all, my day cannot possibly be just one long temper tantrum, can it? The answer is (d)—all of the above and more. A description of my typical day might seem a bit boring, but I think it would help you see my life more clearly because as much as I do not want to be identified by a disease, in effect this disease has a very definite impact on my daily life. You can be forgiven if the following description makes your scalp crawl with impatience. Just skip to the end.

My day begins about an hour before I need to get out of bed. In that hour, I do modified yoga stretches and breathing exercises, followed by a period of meditation. My meditation ends when I see Cristiana's cheerful face poking through my bedroom door. She helps me wash and dress and use my new breathing machine (more on breathing later). She makes my breakfast and I sit down to eat, read the newspaper, and—of primary importance—complete the daily Sudoku.

Late morning is usually spent at my computer, e-mailing friends and taking care of other business. At some point, Cristiana makes my lunch and sets it up for me before she leaves the house for the day. So in the early afternoon, I eat my lunch and lie down for an hour, usually sleeping. I wake up and use the breathing machine. Late afternoons, I spend writing. In the early evening, a friend or Cristiana makes dinner. We eat together and Cristiana helps me get ready for bed, including yet more air. I am in bed, tethered to my BiPAP, reading, by nine o'clock. That's my day.

I try to get out of the house at least three times a week. Various wonderful friends have learned how to load me and my wheelchair into their cars. They have infinite patience in wheeling me around wherever I need to or would like to go. We go to the movies, seemingly endless doctor's appointments, shopping, walks in the park. I seem to have about a two-hour window of energy.

Managing me and my wheelchair is just one of the myriad logistical aspects of my day. I use a walker to get around the house. My progress by foot is so slow that Galen has taken to commenting, somewhere in the midst of my walk between kitchen and office: "Are we there yet? Are we there yet?" Makes me laugh every time. It takes me two hours just to get up in the morning. And that's with help!

You know how busy people often say that they long to slow down? With me, there is no hurry, ever. I used to find this frustrating. But I guess over time I have just gotten used to it. I am doing things now I would never have imagined possible. This reminds me of that old

Lily Tomlin joke: "I used to tell people that when I grew up I wanted to be someone. Now I see I needed to be more specific." In my case, I used to tell people I couldn't slow down. I had too much to do. Now I see I needed to stop kidding myself. Slow . . . is . . . good.

And every now and then, I have a day like October 14th, the day of the ALS walk. As ordered, the day was clear and sunny if a bit chilly. A perfect fall day. I had on my special socks, and Jean and I drove up to Wakefield to meet the rest of the team. By 10 o'clock, everyone was assembled (Galen, Colin, Owen, Gopi/Lora, Poppy, Andrew, Jean, Bill, and three of Galen's friends from work). I was pushed, like the queen herself, three and a half miles around the lake that dominates the center of Wakefield. We talked and laughed. We all agreed that the name of my team (a very lame "Go Team Royce") would absolutely have to be changed. A new name, Viper Squadron, was unanimously agreed upon. That's what happens when you hang out with your kids and their friends—they allow you to feel hip.

After the walk, Jean managed to get me home before I fell sound asleep. Nothing like an extreme dose of fresh air! And as I was sleeping, Galen came home. I awoke to a cup of tea and a suggestion: Let's go to the movies! Every corpuscle in my body demanded that I be reasonable. I try to limit myself, based on past experience, to one outing a day—the previously mentioned two-hour window. But Galen is irresistible. So off we went to see "Little Miss Sunshine," a wonderful movie. On the way home, Galen picked up a pizza. *(Please, do not tell Dr. Joshi I ate a pizza!)*. As we sat eating and watching yet another movie, I suddenly started to shut down. Galen hustled me into bed and I was asleep before she turned out the light. What a great day. I was exhausted for three days afterwards, but it was worth it. So, a profound thank you to everyone who made that day so great. The team raised over $1000; we had a delightful time; the socks were a big hit.

I am discovering something that should come as no surprise. My mental state is very dependent on the condition of my breathing. That's what "As the BiPAP Blows" has been all about. Last week a new episode was added to this ongoing series. We'll call this new episode "The Breathing Gods Descend." A new BiPAP, called a Biflex, arrived and I immediately slept better because, although I am still swallowing air, I'm not swallowing as much air. Amazing what progress looks like, yes?

Then, more progress: a whole new machine has been added to my breathing arsenal. It's called a Cough Assist. I use the Cough Assist three times a day and it is truly wonderful to feel my lungs expand fully again.

Did you know that on any given day most of us take between 75 and 150 deep breaths? Well, we do, and doing so maintains and restores our energy. I no longer have the muscles to do this. The result is rapid energy depletion, so much so that by mid-afternoon even the smallest physical effort feels impossible; my fatigue often reduces me to helpless weeping. However, the BiPap and the Cough Assist reestablish my ability to breathe fully and effectively. More robust energy equals a better attitude, a more optimistic outlook. Since my last update, this has been a real blessing.

Writing the rest of this update has given me time to contemplate further the topic I started with: the realization that I am not going to get my life back. I am not going to get my life back. When this thought first occurred, I felt panicky. Logically, I expected to be devastated. Briefly, I was. Even now, I cannot say the words without choking up. Nonetheless, I also feel—to a much greater degree than grief—relief.

This feeling quite surprised me; I was completely unprepared for a sensation of lightness. I had put something to rest, something that had held me back. Now I could get on with my life. Of course, I wish that I had been given this understanding earlier. But everything has its time. I can only conclude that my anger was a prelude to this new insight. In fact, anger may be its gatekeeper.

Scott finally left for Iraq on September 30th. His current assignment is more perilous than previous ones, and he's able to communicate less frequently. I have to keep reminding myself of the times, earlier in our marriage, when he was in the bush in Nigeria or Liberia or the jungle in Indonesia. He would be gone for months and we would have no means of communication. In recent years, I've grown accustomed to hearing from him by phone or e-mail every few days. But this new assignment makes me anxious. His Internet access is almost nonexistent. When he calls, there is a two second time delay between when he speaks and when I hear him. He tells me they are mortared nightly.

When I spoke with him on Saturday, he told me that the work is finished and now the real work begins—getting out of Iraq. It seems ironic that it is easy to get into Iraq and very difficult to get out. He believes it will take him the better part of this week to negotiate exit transportation for himself and his team. If all goes well, he will leave Kuwait on Friday and arrive home the same day.

We believe this will be Scott's last trip to Iraq. And the congregation says "Amen."

All my love,
Catherine

28 November 2006

Dear Ones,

Imagine this! National Public Radio accepted my essay! (The draft appeared at the end of my September 3rd update.) We recorded it at my house a month ago. Richard Knox expertly handled the recording equipment and Jay Allison encouraged me through headphones. There was so much ambient urban sound that morning—dogs, crows, sound trucks (three days before election day), people, cars, etc.—that it was like dodging raindrops to get the final recording. But it was fun to do, and now you will get to hear the results.

The piece will air on Monday morning, December 4th, on "Morning Edition", on your local NPR affiliate. In Boston, it's WBUR. It will be part of the "This I Believe" series. It will also be on the "This I Believe" web site (*www.thisIbelieve.org*). So you will be able to hear the essay and also to read it. And if that's not enough, you'll also be able to see a photograph of yours truly. How can you miss?

The NPR publication created a murmur of excitement around the old homestead. But this excitement is secondary to our unmitigated joy at having Scott home safely from Iraq. As you know from my last update, this trip was considerably more precarious than previous ones. In fact, the day after Scott and his team were driven cross-country from Basra to Kuwait, the remainder of his project was shut down until further notice for safety reasons. As if to underscore the seriousness of the situation, the week after Scott's exodus, four members of the security team that had ensured his safe passage were killed traveling the same route. Our hearts go out to the families of these men. We are indebted to them for Scott's safe return. Now, we hope his Iraq adventures are over.

In the midst of this, I have been having further adventures of my own. Have you already suspected that this has something to do with the BiPAP? Yes, just when I thought "As the BiPAp Blows" had resolved into happy oblivion, there was a new wrinkle. The Biflex was a good idea as far as it went, but it was unable to manage the carbon dioxide buildup in my blood. The imbalance occurred so gradually, I was unaware of it until it precipitated a crisis. One night, almost three weeks ago, I was sleeping very fitfully, waking up every hour or so, sweating and gasping for air. Then, in the middle of the night, like a red alarm button being pushed in my brain, I suddenly believed I was suffocating. For the rest of the night, in spite of all my attempts at reason, I battled against a terrifying and overwhelming panic.

For months now, I have worked with myself to calm the panic that comes, usually in the middle of the night, when I imagine the future. I urge these thoughts to come back at another time, a better time. "A better time" is another way of saying "never." But what I had actually been doing was putting these thoughts into a box. The night I believed I was suffocating, the lid blew off the box. It exploded.

The contents of the box became creatures that flew to the dark corners of my bedroom. There, from the gloom, they waited with arrows cocked in their bows. During that night, every time I seemed to get myself calmed down, another arrow would come zinging at me from a new corner. In the end, I felt powerless to protect myself. The only thing I seemed to know for certain was that I would be safe when the sun came up.

The sun came up, and I slept. But I did not recover. During the two days following, I was besieged by headaches and nausea. Finally, the physical pain, like a tsunami subsiding, left behind wreckage. Even as I tell you about this now, the anxiety returns. I feel as though something has entered the deepest, most intimate and private parts of my being, thrown the furniture around, blown holes in the walls, floor and ceiling, and smashed the lights. This place that I had previously come to rely upon as safe, I now enter fearfully, afraid that a false step will send me hurtling into oblivion. Did I mention I had experienced a crisis?

And yet in the midst of these dark and terrible moments, I also had a vision. It happened during a cranio-sacral session earlier that same night. One of the hallmarks of cranio-sacral work is bringing one's attention to what they call "sensation." In this session, my forehead felt cold, as if I were resting it against stone. I imagined myself lying on my stomach on a marble floor. My arms were above my head, my legs stretched long on the floor, my toes pointed, as if I were a diver in midair. Suddenly, an enormous golden man appeared at my head. He flung a blanket across me made of millions of gold stars. Glaring fiercely around the room, he declared, "She is under my protection." He seemed to be warning away anyone who did not have my best interests at heart.

In the middle of that night, as the arrows flew, I remember thinking, "God, if this is your protection, please do better." I felt utterly abandoned. But in the days that followed, I became aware of how extraordinary that starry blanket truly was. Some might call the stars "resources." I call them blessings: my beloved husband, devoted friends, inspired therapists, a skilled acupuncturist, a caring medical team, and my meditation master. They all sat with me, talked with me, held my hand, brought me exquisite gifts, while I awaited the greatest healer of all-time. Almost three weeks later, I can describe the episode without reliving its horror. And yet, something at my core has been shaken. I am emotionally frail now in a way I have never been before. I trust that with the passage of time, I will regain my strength. In fact, with time, I believe I will be even stronger.

In the meantime, I have reverted to the old BiPAP machine. It's working as well as can be expected, and I have added some helpful pharmaceuticals to my arsenal. The special cookies were fun, but who could imagine that in a college town, supply would be an issue? Also, I discovered that the quality was not uniform. (Surprise, surprise!) So I have turned to something more reliable. An experience like that night is worth doing once. But I do not intend to repeat it.

Finally, I come to one of the greatest blessings of the past few months: Cristiana. The unfortunate news is that she was not able to metriculate into a master's program here in Boston, so she will return to Italy tomorrow. I will miss her keenly. She has been a consistent bright light for me and for everyone in my household, since the moment she walked through our door. We send her home with grateful hearts and wish her every blessing. The good news is that having experienced Cristiana, I now know exactly what I am looking for. I am hoping that some of you will be able to help me find the new Cristiana. As you may recall, we found her because my sister Becket spammed her e-mail list on my behalf. Her request went to a friend outside Boston. That friend forwarded the request to selected members of her church congregation, one of whom knew Cristiana.

We are looking for someone to come and live with us and, in exchange for room and board, help me for about 20 hours a week. If you would like to be part of the new e-mail chain that reveals the new Cristiana, please let me know and I will send more details.

This has been an eventful time. I wrote the radio essay just before Scott left for Iraq, shortly before Cristiana came to live with us, and before my dark night. Now, Scott is home. Cristiana is leaving. I am recovering. I would not change a word of the essay.

All my love,
Catherine

14 December 2006

Dear Ones,

There's a sort of origin myth—well, a story anyway—that helps to explain my current take on life. Recently, I found myself telling it to a friend, and it occurs to me now that this might be a good time to share it with all of you. I'm a big fan of stories.

My story even has a title: "I Asked for Liberation in This Lifetime And God Sent Me to the Home Depot." Cool title, no? I always meant to write a book to go with it but never got around to it. As many as you know, I worked for a brief time at the Home Depot. But that's not where the story begins. It actually begins the summer before I made the rather counterintuitive decision to put my MBA and 30 years of business experience to work selling flooring in the big orange box store.

That summer, I was participating in a weeklong meditation retreat, something I have enjoyed doing for many years. It was toward the end of the week and my restlessness and complaints had finally been replaced by a sense of peace and well-being. During a break, I was talking quietly with one of the participants when he quoted for me a line of scripture about the role of the spiritual seeker. I can no longer remember what the line was. Even at the time, I had to ask him to repeat it twice just to hold onto it long enough to digest it. But, as someone pointed out recently, once you have the fish, you no longer need to think about the hook. And so the line of scripture is lost, but from that moment, my life was never quite the same.

The scripture was about the purpose of a human life. Previously, I had always thought that we are here for many reasons: to be an artist, to raise children, to be a banker, to find cures for diseases, etc. But at that moment I came to understand that we are all here for one purpose only. Whether we know it or not, whether we care about it or not, whether we believe it or not, we are here to know God. Every path we tread leads to this same place.

One of my favorite thoughts comes from the medieval theologian Meister Eckhardt: "The eyes with which I see God are the same eyes with which God sees me." This is the purpose of a human life, to experience God fully and without reservation, and to understand through that experience than we are all God. Your understanding of God may be quite different. There is no right or wrong here. But when this realization settled into me, I knew that, for me, this was a complete and ultimate truth.

The retreat site had a temple. It was a beautiful and deeply quiet place, and that's where I went. With my new understanding, I went to see what would happen next. As soon as I sat down, cross-legged on the blue carpet, the words of my new understanding presented themselves again. I heard myself say, silently, "The purpose of a human life is only and always to know God." And then I heard myself say, again silently, "Well, then let's get on with it!"

That moment completely rearranged every molecule of my intention for my life. Before, I'm not sure I could have said what exactly my intention was. To be a good person? To be a good wife, a good mother, a good friend? To be smart, or to make a contribution? Afterward, I knew that knowing God would include all of that and much more. The expression "there's more" has always been the hallmark of my life, so how could I *not* commit to pursuing the ultimate "there's more?"

Perhaps many of you are saying in the back of your minds, "Catherine, watch out what you ask for!" I am defining *liberation* in this experience in the classic sense of ultimate unity with the divine. By agreeing to "get on with it," I was asking to experience this unity before I die. At the time, I did not know that the timetable for my death was already engaged. This retreat happened in the summer of 2000.

By the end of that summer, I was aware that my job as a small business consultant had been causing great stress and no joy. My tolerance for such a life came to an end. I began to look around, broadening my gaze to include jobs that had never occurred to me before. I realized that somehow I made it out of my teens without ever working in retail. *Retail,* I thought. Now that would be novel. I listed all the places I like to shop. It was a very short list. I don't like to shop. But an inventory of my shopping habits revealed one place I truly did like to shop: The Home Depot. I loved the products. I loved the smell, especially the smell of sawdust. I even liked the orange.

There's a whole story about the day I sat in the parking lot outside the Home Depot in Quincy, Massachusetts, and summoned up the courage to walk inside and apply for a job. The important point is I got the job. I worked there for a year before my reputation as a whiz at selling flooring got out and I was recruited to Lowe's. However, just as I was beginning to make the transition from one big hardware store to another, I noticed that the muscles in my left hand were beginning to act strangely. It was 2001 and these were the first flutterings of ALS.

Around the time I started at the Home Depot, I was introduced to the phrase "uninterrupted loving service." Needless to say, this phrase was not part of the Home Depot new hire training! It came from another source entirely. Immediately, my imagination was captivated by it, probably because it seemed so hopelessly impossible to perform. I thought I would dedicate that year at Home Depot to exploring this concept at work and at home.

It was at work that I experienced the challenges most graphically. In fact, in a setting like The Home Depot, theory and polite inquiry are replaced by hard-core practical experience virtually overnight. My department was chronically understaffed. Apparently, when you show up at The Home Depot looking for a job and you have an advanced degree on your résumé, they put you in flooring. Maybe they figure you can do the math. Or they figure all that education must give you good taste. Whatever the reason, it seems that not too many people with advanced degrees think of going to work at The Home Depot.

So my idea of uninterrupted loving service was immediately slapped around by the realities of too few employees serving too many customers in too short a time. When you put grain through a mill, the result is fine understanding. I learned that uninterrupted loving service is synonymous with compassion. I learned three important things about compassion that year. Compassion and pity are mutually exclusive. Compassion is not the same thing as making everybody happy all the time. And, I cannot have compassion for others before having compassion for myself. Therefore, the uninterrupted loving service I strive to offer, I must offer first and foremost to myself. From that place of deep loving, my well of compassion for others can seem limitless.

It's not that I learned it all that year. I'm still learning it. It's just that during that year the foundation for a new way of living and relating to the world was laid. Does this mean that, given my current circumstances, I never feel pity for myself? Oh, Lord, I wish that were true! Alas, I am no paragon of forbearance and optimism. I can feel sorry for myself with the best of them. Ask Scott! But after that Home Depot year, I knew there was more to it. I learned that when indulging in my own woes, I need to take a step back and see my whole life, with its great beauty and daily delights and surprises.

One of the ongoing delights and surprises is this: Even though every day I can do less and less to make people happy, the world keeps going around. No longer able to take care of others, I had thought life would lose its meaning. In fact, I had thought that no one would care for me. Of course, this could not be further from the truth. Life goes on and I go on with it.

Every step I take, every moment of every day, every decision I make, takes me closer to knowing God.

On a practical note, today we are anxiously awaiting the arrival of my power wheelchair. It has been promised for almost two months. A friend who has used a wheelchair for over 30 years told me the other day, when I expressed reluctance about switching over to the chair, "Catherine, walking is highly overrated." I fall more often now and I find walking from one room to another utterly exhausting. So I guess he must be right. Now that I think about it, every physical transition I have been through in the last three years has come at exactly the right moment. So rather than fight the change, I will try to embrace it with a grateful heart. So, come on wheelchair! Timing in life is, indeed, everything.

Also, as you may have guessed, I am feeling much better, physically and mentally. The shattered room I described in my last update turns out to be less important to my sense of safety and well-being than

I'd first thought. It's where I went to calm myself down when I felt vulnerable or scared. The room image is gone now; I'll just have to be scared right out there in public. If that includes some unsightly crying, I'll get used to it.

Something else is about to happen, something that had seemed unlikely to happen again. The day after Christmas, Scott will leave for Iraq one more time. This time he is scheduled to be gone only there weeks and there will be no overland travel. Nonetheless, Mama ain't happy.

At the moment, we are advertising for a new personal care assistant. Perhaps because of the holidays, we have had no responses so far. Cristiana spoiled me thoroughly. It has been a difficult couple of weeks without her. How we will manage with Scott in Iraq remains to be revealed.

As most of you know, my NPR radio essay went off splendidly. I can say that immodestly because once I had written and recorded it, the rest was entirely out of my hands. Special thanks to all those who wrote to tell me you had heard it. As I was recording it, the thought occurred to me that the essay was a gift. I am happy to hear the gift has been received.

Scott, Galen, Owen and I wish all of you a very joyful time in the next few weeks in pursuit of whatever you celebrate at this time of year.

All my love,
Catherine

Part Four

14 February 2007   Happy Valentine's Day!

Dear Ones,

Ananda. It's a Sanskrit word that means bliss. I was reminded recently that even in the midst of despair there is always bliss.

Ananda. The word has a gentle urgency to it. I remind myself of it as often as I can.

Ananda. I have been told that Sanskrit words often carry a unique vibration, a signature energy.

Ananda. In the middle of the night when I wake up wondering, first thing in the morning when every molecule feels out of place, late in the afternoon when I feel I've lost my way, I say this word.

It helps.

Ananda. I offer it to you as a reminder or perhaps something totally new. Bliss is ours. When I go looking for bliss, I find it in my heart.

The vapor trail following my NPR essay has been rich. I have heard from old friends from around the world. I have heard from complete strangers, some a little stranger than others. There has been much poignancy, some joy, and a little comedy.

For example, I received a call from someone who had gone to a great deal of trouble to locate my telephone number. She began by saying she was praying for me. I thanked her. She then proceeded to ask for my e-mail address because she had some research, involving consuming large quantities of raw vegetables, that she wanted to send me. I thanked her again, but declined.

"Well," she shot back. "I'll still pray for you!"

That's what I like, prayer as threat. Several days later, I received a card in the mail from her enclosing a brochure for the "Campus Crusade for Christ." I'm all set now, thanks.

This must be my 15 minutes of fame. The essay has been translated into at least three languages: French, Chinese, and Vietnamese. One of my alma maters picked it up as an alumna tidbit. Several blogs also picked it up, my absolute favorite of which is a woman in New York City who followed my essay with the closing monologue from the movie "Trainspotting." In case you've forgotten, it's a rather random and somewhat demented riff on choice.* I loved it!

And for what I trust will be a brief time, I have become a minor poster girl for ALS. I am now in the process of responding to an interview with the national ALS Association. I figure once I complete this interview, I will have said pretty much everything I came here to say. Of course, it's anyone's guess what will actually turn up in print. One of the things I learned from all those years in Boston City Hall is that you can control what you say, but you cannot control what they hear (and print).

In the meantime, Scott, once again, pulled one out of his hat and got home safely from Iraq. How much longer he continues to do this work is anyone's guess. I have given up trying to extract promises of no return. I want him here at home, but, more importantly, don't want him *there*. My physical condition will require his uninterrupted presence here soon enough. That imperative can speak for me when the time comes.

However, we're not there yet. Right now we're celebrating the arrival of Mariana, my new PCA. She just graduated from medical school in Brazil and has come to the States to improve her English and begin the process of qualifying for a residency here. She's a lovely young woman, and we all look forward to enjoying each other's company for at least the next six months.

The drama of "As the BiPAP Blows" is, mercifully, in hiatus. The replacement drama is a search for a van that can transport me and my magnificent new wheelchair. It's been bloody cold here, so I haven't wanted to go out much. Nevertheless, I'm as restless as a teenager. I need wheels, man. Thanks to the wheelchair ramp, I can now leave the house and wander the neighborhood on my own steam, but trips beyond my immediate universe are fraught with difficulties. You know, Jane, there's always something . . .

We are in the depths of winter. Our first major snowstorm is expected tonight. But after 5 p.m., it is still light. Scott swears he smelled spring in the air the other day. When we first moved into our house 30 years ago, I planted a rhododendron under the front window. It's grown large and healthy but its leaves are shriveled and shrunken from the cold, and I know that spring is still a ways off.

Even now, *ananda*.

All my love,
Catherine

Monologue from Trainspotting:

"Choose Life. Choose a job. Choose a career. Choose a family. Choose a fucking big television, choose washing machines, cars, compact disc players and electrical tin openers. Choose good health, low cholesterol, and dental insurance. Choose fixed interest mortgage repayments. Choose a starter home. Choose your friends. Choose leisurewear and matching luggage. Choose a three-piece suite on hire purchase in a range of fucking fabrics. Choose DIY and wondering who the fuck you are on a Sunday morning. Choose sitting on that couch watching mind-numbing, spirit-crushing game shows, stuffing fucking junk food into your mouth. Choose rotting away at the end of it all, pishing your last in a miserable home, nothing more than an embarrassment to the selfish, fucked up brats you spawned to replace yourself.

Choose your future.
Choose life.

20 March 2007

Dear Ones,

There was one other consequence of my NPR essay. A few weeks after it aired, I was approached by a literary agent. He believed, as many of you have suggested, that these updates were a potential book. It got me thinking. I have real misgivings about embarking on a book project. My time is precious and energy limited. It seems likely that turning my attention to a book would require that I put aside other things, most notably, these updates. Intuitively, I have felt that continuing the updates was more important.

Fortunately, at that same time I happened to meet someone who confirmed my intuition. The publisher of a small press, he agreed to read what I've written so far and give his honest assessment. He had the grace and fortitude to read all of the updates, and this was his conclusion: There is no book. Why? Because I'm not finished and the updates are a work in progress. Let me tell you, my relief is considerable.

Besides, I feel surprisingly comfortable in this state of *becoming*. The latter part of my dance career was devoted to improvisational performance. My colleagues and I would step out onto the stage having no set choreography. We allowed ourselves to respond to the impetus of the moment, making the dance intimate and immediate. When this worked well, it created a union between dancer and audience that was truly magical. It didn't always work well, but that's what made it seem so exciting, almost death defying. Everything was always a work in progress.

I have returned to those thrilling days of yesteryear through these updates. Recently, my friend who sends me wonderful socks sent me a pair with "dancer" stamped all over them. At first she was afraid that the word *dancer* would be a painful reminder of something that has been taken from me. But way back when, she was one of my improvisation partners. She knows that I will always be a dancer. But now I dance with words and with you. When I start to write to you, I am never sure what is going to come out. The invitation to make a complete fool of myself is always open, but so, too, is the opportunity for something magical.

All of this brings me to two things I have been thinking about lately. They have to do with attachment. They seem like two arms of a giant smiling octopus, somewhat Disneyesque, but not entirely benign. They both have to do with love. One is about how I love myself and the other is about how I love others, specifically my most perfect love, Scott. The manner in which I experience these two types of love is being seriously challenged. Quite simply, I can no longer have them the way I used to. For 58 years, I have defined and refined what it means to love myself. For 35 of those years, Scott has taught me how deeply and fully I can love another. Like most people at my age, I thought I had it pretty well worked out.

But no. I had no idea the degree to which it was important to me to manage the minutia of my life—until I no longer could. There's nothing like needing someone else to help you go to the bathroom for the edges of your world to get fuzzy. Knowing that this day would come, I had imagined unbearable humiliation. Now that it's here, it just is. I thought I would somehow have to love myself less to accommodate such a change. I discovered quite the opposite. I have to love myself more. Not only that, I have the capacity to love myself more. Maybe not more, maybe *better*. But giving up and moving on from my former way of loving myself has been painful.

My day is filled now with all sorts of accommodations. Much to my chagrin, I have discovered heretofore unimaginable levels of self absorption. Frankly folks, it's all about me. The horror! I spend inordinate amounts of time worrying that things I can no longer do will not get done as I would like. Of course, it goes without saying that my way is the best way, the only way. So I worry. I am frustrated. Sometimes I am overwhelmed by fear and foreboding. I have panic attacks.

Just as I felt myself hurtling into the greedy arms of anxiety a few nights ago, a gentle voice made a suggestion. It said, simply: "Catherine, make your mind your friend." It was perfect advice, perfectly timed. I spoke to my mind as if I were speaking to a loved one. I invited it to think of something pleasant, something soothing, something loving. I presented it with a couple of possible scenarios to get started. Immediately, my breathing deepened and I became calm. Shortly, I drifted off to sleep.

The next morning, I pondered: What had happened? A reminder. I seem to need this reminder constantly: Nothing is more powerful than love. These days, forgetting this simple message is an unhealthy indulgence. It's an attachment to a sense of myself that was convenient, but now no longer serves. Most of my life I have believed that in the realm of unconquerable might, love was a poor, weak stepchild. These habitual ways of thinking are so strong. Replacing them with something more beneficial takes practice, practice, practice. You'll find me in the practice room a lot these days.

Scott's closest high school friend was killed in Vietnam. A few years ago, Scott went to visit his grave. Through the intervening years, Scott had often mentioned to me the great loss he felt with the death of this friend. Standing there in the cemetery, Scott finally understood why. This was Scott's first true friendship. In the presence of this friend, Scott experienced great love and affection. Scott equated losing the friend with losing access to that ability to love. Standing beside his grave, Scott realized that the love was still very much alive in him and always had been. Nothing had been lost except the ready reminder in the form of his friend.

Something is going on now that, at first, surprised me. As my life is so manifestly winding down, my loved ones are leaving me even before I leave them. In a very healthy and natural way, they are getting on with their lives. Galen is planning for medical school. Owen is looking forward to going to Sweden to help open a restaurant. Scott is going to Iraq again and again and looking forward to other opportunities for fulfilling work. This all feels exciting and wonderful. Except when it doesn't.

I am fortunate. I married someone whom I have grown to love and respect. In Scott's presence, I experience profound and even mystifying love. When he goes away, I feel convinced that he takes that love with him, and I am bereft. But I am learning, just as Scott learned with his friend, that this love is not transitory. It is not dependent upon another's physical presence. Once again, at the risk of repeating myself, it's all about me. All this time, I thought my love was a gift to Scott. In fact, it has been a gift to myself which can never be taken away.

So as I ache for the physical presence of my beloved, I can bathe in that love and feel comforted and content. I ache because I am accustomed to equating his presence with his love. When I break that attachment, I am awed to discover the love remains. The discipline lies in remembering.

In the past year and a half I've been getting lots of reminders. Scott left for Iraq again two days ago and will be gone for a couple of weeks. This, I begin to understand, is the gift these trips of his offer. I am fearful and fretful initially, but soon realize that I am missing the point. Scott's trips to Iraq are not a mistake or some terrible injustice. They are an opportunity to become more firmly at peace with myself in the life I have been given.

Although the weather has been mild, this feels like the end of an extraordinarily long winter. Today we have snow on the ground and little green shoots poking up. I'll admit to just a touch of cabin fever. But mobility is at hand! Tomorrow or the next day at the latest, I will become the proud owner of a 1998 Dodge handicap van. The folks at Ayers Handicap have gone well beyond the call in setting up this van. They not only found the van but did all of the legwork necessary to get it inspected, registered, insured and in top working order. I cannot say enough good things about them. First stop in the new van? The annual New England Flower Show. Give me green! I have not missed the show in almost 30 years.

I also have a new cast of characters coming through the house. Almost every day now, I am visited by various care givers who want to ensure my continued good health. It's time-consuming, but also nurtures peace of mind and allows me to anticipate the inevitable challenges that lie ahead. For example, certainly by this summer, I will need to have a feeding tube surgically implanted in my stomach. In the past, I have referred to ALS as an untreatable illness. This is not entirely accurate. My BiPAp, and whatever other future breathing support may be necessary, and the feeding tube are treatments, not end-of-life interventions. They allow me to stay as healthy as possible for as long as possible. They are choices.

I also have the wonderful company of my children and close friends. As I said, I am loved and well cared for. The other day a friend came to visit. She had been staying away because she had had a bad cold. Much to my horror, she had already gone home after her visit with me before I realized I had never asked her how she was feeling. I seem to do this a lot now—forget that I am not alone. I suspect that's how I will know that I have turned some kind of corner—when my self-obsession fades and I become aware of others again. I'm looking forward to it. Perhaps you are, too? If so, thank you for your current forbearance.

All my love,
Catherine

27 April 2007

Dear Ones,

First, some headlines:

On May 20, Galen will once again be participating in the fund-raising bike ride for ALS. As she did last year, she is welcoming sponsors and co-riders. With any luck, I will be there too.

On May 3, I will acquiesce to the fine counsel of my doctors and family and spend a couple of days in Mass General having a G-tube inserted into my stomach. The surgery itself is not considered a big deal. They just need to keep me under observation until they're sure the tube is working well and delivering nourishment. In the end, my level of nutrition should improve and with it my energy and sense of well-being. Given how laborious eating—chewing, swallowing, getting the food to my mouth—has become, this should really be a blessing.

My NPR essay continues to be like a pebble in still water. Even now, I am receiving forwarded e-mails from people who are just now hearing the essay. I have also been adopted by the ALS Association, which has published a profile of me on their national web site.

Last Sunday, I had the good fortune to speak before a couple hundred people at a local symposium hosted by the ALS Association. It was a fun but exhausting undertaking. Afterwards, I immediately came down with a raging head cold. Nonetheless, I'm going to share with you what I shared with them because it speaks to where I am at the moment and is the best update I've got.

LIVING WITH ALS

Living with ALS. Well, here we are, doing just that. We're in it.

Recently one of my docs had the occasion to refer to me as a "basket case." Don't you just hate it when medical people talk down to you? Use those big, technical medical terms? Basket case.

And he was right. I was a basket case. I was overwhelmed by all of the things that so easily overwhelm us:

What will the next stage of my illness be like?
Who is going to take care of me?
How will we afford to pay for caregivers?
Will I ever again get a good night's sleep?
Will I decide yes or no to a G-tube?

Little things like that.

I have a rule that I try to hold to. When I sense myself feeling overwhelmed, I try to bring myself back to the present moment. Generally speaking, when I'm feeling anxious, it's because I'm worrying about something that may or may not happen in the future. By focusing on the present moment, I can calm myself down because usually what's happening right now, in this exact moment, is okay. Like this moment, here, right now.

There are times, however, when the present and future appear to collide.

That's what seems to have been happening for me lately. So I was very grateful when two people whom I trust, two people who don't even know each other, gave me the same bit of advice.

I believe that life is all about choice. Even as my body is doing this thing I would rather it weren't, I am still the one, and the only one, who gets to decide how I feel about it. Sometimes it's hard to remember this when it seems like everyone around me is telling me what a rotten deal I've been handed. But the truth is, it's only rotten if I agree it is.

I'm no Pollyanna. On some days it's hard to hold on to a sense of hope and optimism. On other days, it's a little easier. And this bit of advice, which I am about to share with you, definitely helps me keep things on the bright side.

The advice is very simple. As I go about my daily life and all of the decisions, large and small, that greet me every day, whenever possible choose comfort. Be comfortable.

I come from generations of hardy New England stock. We don't choose comfort. We are independent. We see a certain amount of suffering as a virtue. If there is a hard way and an easy way, we're apt to choose the hard way because we believe it builds moral fiber. Choose comfort? I think not.

I have had ALS for six years. I must not be the brightest bulb in the box because it has taken me almost all that time to realize that there's enough moral fiber building in ALS, all by itself. There is no reason in the world why I need to add to it by making decisions that make my life more difficult. Be comfortable.

I really had to think about this, so foreign is it to my nature. I thought about my life: physical, mental and spiritual.

What does it mean to choose to be physically comfortable? Well, that seemed like the easy question. Catherine, if you can't sleep, take something that will help you get there. I was always one of those people who hesitated to take an aspirin. Well, that's definitely a thing of the past now. My little bedtime pharmaceutical cocktail is a welcome friend. For a moment, I actually heard myself ask my doc, "But couldn't this be habit forming?" Right.

What does it mean to choose to be mentally comfortable? When my husband and I got married, we got that classic advice: "Never go to bed mad." My new advice is "Never go to bed fretting." If there is something on my mind at bedtime, resolve it right then or promise to resolve it in the morning. I've learned that absolutely nothing ever gets resolved once the lights go out.

Also, I find myself less and less able to make myself do things I genuinely do not want to do. I no longer feel obligated to see people I don't want to see, read things that don't interest me (especially all those "inspirational" books people can't seem to resist sending), go places I don't want to go, or even answer the phone every time it rings. By the way, I have found that the people I most want to see are the ones who do not pity me. In fact, I have developed an absolute aversion to people who approach me, faces pulled down sorrowfully, voices dripping with funereal sincerity, and ask, "How are you?" I always feel compelled to respond, through gritted teeth, "Fine. Just fine."

What does it mean to choose to be spiritually comfortable? Well, first of all it means knowing beyond a shadow of a doubt that ALS is not some punishment that I have been dealt because of past misdeeds. God is not angry with me. In fact, by disciplining myself to choose comfort, the greatest comfort I receive comes from my faith. In the dark of night when, despite my best efforts, I am still fretting, I turn the fretting into a conversation with God. Every one of us has our own version of God (including the absolute belief that there is no God). My version believes that God and I are one. So when I speak lovingly and compassionately and honestly to myself, I am touching the comfort that faith has to offer. I do this more often now.

Choose comfort. It's not a form of self-indulgence. We have ALS, for crying out loud. We need to give ourselves a break. We need to love ourselves, as we are, completely. Happiness is our birthright. By choosing comfort we choose a kind of special defiance. We will not allow this illness to rob us of our joy.

✳✳

That was the end of my talk. I believe what I said in the talk with my whole heart. One might be forgiven for assuming that I am therefore content and at one with what is happening to me. The truth, however, is something entirely different.

I find myself rereading my own published words and wondering why I am not experiencing the solace I write about. In fact, I have to admit that I am deeply depressed, and finding every day a long, uphill climb. I feel overwhelmed and unable to cope. For the first time in my life, I feel at the bottom of a pit I can't get out of.

My attitude has lost some altitude. Hope for elevation seems to lie in two areas at the moment. One is the G-tube which should increase my caloric intake (I am now at 113 pounds and falling) and therefore boost my energy. The second is success in locating an effective antidepressant. This is all in the works and I am optimistic. I've never taken an antidepressant before, so there's a whole learning curve that goes with this. I had no idea how complicated it could be. For one thing, I have discovered that the wrong one can leave you feeling worse than you felt before. Now, how is that fair?

At the same time, we have turned a corner in the level of care I require. Until now, the loving attentions of family and friends have perfectly met my needs. Now, for my safety and the safety of my loved ones, I need consistent help from a person trained to support someone in my circumstances. In Boston, this presents a mighty challenge. A reliable, well-trained, experienced personal care attendant (PCA) is a cherished commodity.

Part of the challenge is paying such a person. My insurance does not cover PCA support. In the grand scheme of things, their hourly rate is by no means exorbitant; it's just more than I have to spend. My dilemma is not unusual. Everyone who is working with me now—my neurological team, the ALS Association, the visiting healthcare people, in short, all of those people who routinely interact with patients just like me—see this dilemma play out again and again. It's the classic middle class conundrum: too rich to qualify for state support and too poor to pay out of pocket. Apparently, there are some legal avenues we can pursue. So that's the next step.

In the midst of all this, Mariana, who has been so extraordinarily good with me, has been offered a fellowship at Harvard Medical School. This means a change in visa status, so she has to return to Brazil almost immediately and for an unspecified length of time. Of course, I am delighted for her; this is a great opportunity. But it does add another layer of complexity here at home.

Thank God, to bolster our spirits, spring has finally arrived. My wheelchair van has a couple of glitches that we're working on. But at the moment, at least, I can take short trips in it, and it's great to get out. Scott is home for the time being.

Sorry to be so "woe is me." Courage, I trust, will return.

All my love,
Catherine

New Posting

PCA for Woman with ALS

Middle-aged woman, wife, mother (grown children), author, living with ALS seeks daytime personal-care attendant in Boston. Primary duties include helping me with the activities of daily living.

I use a wheelchair and have limited use of my hands. I need another pair of hands to help with such tasks as dressing, preparing food, administering and cleaning my breathing equipment (simple, will train), toileting and minor household chores such as watering plants and doing laundry. Occasionally cook dinner. No housecleaning.

I have an extensive network of family and friends to support me, but need 2 consistent people on whom I can rely.

Position 1: Live out

Monday through Friday—9am-5pm paid position. ($12/hr), prior PCA experience preferred.

Position 2: Live in

Monday through Friday—5pm-8pm and Sunday 1pm-5pm. Your assistance in exchange for room and board in large Victorian house. Private room and shared bathroom. Previous experience assisting someone with a disability would be helpful, and you must have prior work experience.

Applicants must be cheerful, dependable, and mature. References (at least 2) are required. Must like dogs.

Parking available—convenient to Redline and bus routes.

Please respond by e-mail to Catherine: roycenagel@aol.com.

27 May 2007

Dear Ones,

Much better. Much, much better. Thank you.

I went into the hospital on May 2nd, really not knowing what to expect. After all, the last time I was in a hospital was 1964. Yes, this means I had my children at home—thus confirming all of those suspicions you've been harboring about me being a secret/closet hippie. So . . . anyway . . . moving right along . . .

The hospital is one of the best in the world—Massachusetts General. The staff was excellent. I had a room with a beautiful, panoramic view of the Charles River and Cambridge beyond. The surgery was performed according to the latest protocols and came off without a hitch. Nonetheless, the entire experience confirmed for me exactly why it has been 43 years since my last hospital stay. I never, ever, want to see the inside of a hospital again.

I don't mean to sound ungrateful. After all, everything went my way. Nonetheless, I was amazed by the degree to which hospitals are not really set up for sick people. If you're sick, you need to rest, right? You need to sleep at night. So why was it necessary to draw arterial blood, a painful process, at four o'clock in the morning? And then there was the rather unsettling experience of waking up to find a flashlight shining in my face. I felt like I was back in summer camp undergoing some initiation rite. But no, it was just the respiration therapist making sure my BiPAp was working properly. Well, when my BiPAp is not working an alarm sounds. I wanted to tell the guy to put the flashlight under his chin, laugh a ghoulish laugh, and let me get back to sleep.

These, however, were just oddities compared with the frustration of being in a room that could not accommodate the little independence I still have. The BiPAp was on a shelf above my head, so I could not manage it on my own. The controls to the bed were inaccessible as well. The bedside table was on the left, a side I can no longer use, so I couldn't even get myself a drink of water. This is where my extraordinarily wonderful daughter came in. She spent both nights sleeping in my wheelchair so that she could do all of the things for me I could not do on my own. Without her, the experience would have been a nightmare. As it was, at every moment, I had a sweet and loving helper. And during the days, I had Scott and Owen. These, and the successful surgery, were my blessings.

Now I have a shiny little white tube discreetly protruding from my side. Through it, I receive a kind of nutrient milkshake four times a day. Today, almost a month into this regimen, I have begun to gain some weight back and am feeling more like myself than I have in months. Nutrition—one of the building blocks of life. Surprise, surprise! In retrospect, I am now becoming aware of the toll several months of nausea and heartburn, and the attendant loss of appetite, had taken on my body. In fact, the week before my surgery, I had given up eating entirely. No wonder I felt so dreadful!

My stamina is still unreliable, but I feel a renewed vitality for which I'm deeply grateful. This allows me to redouble my efforts on what I refer to as "The Bookends Project," otherwise known as "Getting My Affairs in Order." One end of the bookends is today: this present moment. The other end is when my todays finally run out, and all the details to prepare for that.

To the latter end, Scott and I are redoing the embarrassingly earnest wills we concocted in the mid-80s. Certain directives are now in place to ensure that no well-meaning medical person prolongs my life through even modest heroism. I am currently making arrangements to donate parts of my body to ALS research. And, of course, I will want to get all of you together to ensure that the party truly does continue after I'm gone. Details of that are being worked out.

All of this may seem a bit grim, but it actually gives me some peace of mind. Out of these preparations, most of which have been done in consultation with Scott and Owen and Galen, has come at least one delightful moment. We were having a conversation about where my ashes should end up. I have never held much stock in tombstones and cemeteries, except as wildlife sanctuaries in disguise. So I was thinking that I would like to scatter my ashes in the orchard I wrote about in my story "Meeting Cathy." But then the observation was made that Cathy might not always own that land in New Hampshire. What then? Owen had the answer.

"Mom, I think you've got it all wrong. I think Dad and Galen and I need to take you on a final trip. I think we should put your ashes in the Ganges."

And so it will be. An Indian friend of ours has already offered to help make this possible. I am delighted at the prospect of my family, all of whom love to travel and have adventures, doing this together with me. It feels right.

And so "The Bookends Project" progresses. In the meantime, I continue to make the daily adjustments that my life requires. I love hearing from all of you. Please forgive me if time goes by before I respond. But know how much it means to me to open my e-mail and find something from one of you. There are times when life seems unnecessarily serious and sad, and you bring in the light. My friend Cheryl recently wrote:

"Man, what do you write to a woman who is way out there on the frontiers of life, battling her way through the jungles, fording uncharted rivers, and blazing a trail into eternity and sending us back emails? Maybe just, dance on!"

I love that.

Now let me introduce the "Four Fabulous Females:" Sarah, Diane, Sheryl and Jean. They have all been featured in these updates in the past. They are dear friends who have come together to help make my life and Scott's life more possible. Inspired by a book called *Share the Care*, they have contacted a wide circle of friends and family, organizing whatever support people can easily and appropriately provide. My gratitude for this is boundless. Scott will soon go away for a couple of weeks. (Texas, not Iraq!) The Four Fabulous Females are already deeply engaged in ensuring that I am completely cared for in his absence.

And they are ably abetted by my new PCA, Pittsma. A third-year nursing student at UMass Boston, she is cheerful, capable, willing, reliable, and very strong—she can lift me! I look forward to seeing her every morning when she comes to get me up. This is the first time we have hired a PCA. She does not live with us, but works for an hourly rate. At the moment, we are still not eligible for insurance to cover the cost.

The process of deciding to have the stomach surgery was instructive. While I am not seeking to prolong my life, I am very much in favor of experiencing as little pain as possible. The surgery has eliminated all of the debilitating symptoms that I now realize were the effects of starving myself. I feel better. The next big deciding point is apt to involve breathing—whether to go on a ventilator or not. But that's down the road. We'll see. In the meantime . . .

Dance on!

All my love,
Catherine

On July 1, 2007, Dorchester neighbors Diane McCormack and Tom Torronto hosted an afternoon fundraising party for Catherine and her family. Dozens of fabulous items were donated for a silent auction, from weekend getaways on Cape Cod to exercise classes to works of art. Thirty guests placed bids at the party, while others from across the country called in their bids. The event raised money to defray medical costs, in particular the cost of a personal care assistant.

7 July 2007

Dear Ones,

Thank you sounds completely inadequate. It's too short, too terse, too facile—just not enough of anything. And yet it's the best I can do to show my gratitude for all the wonderful people who honored me with their presence last Sunday. The Four Fabulous Females throw a fantastic party. About 30 of you were there, and I was deeply moved by the depth and history I have with everyone who came. There were also many who could not come but who were waiting in the wings. Thank you all for the greatness of your love.

This update is long-overdue. One aspect of voice recognition software is less than ideal: When I write, others can listen in. Ever since my surgery, my house has been filled by a daily rotation of medical people: nurses, home health aides, occupational and physical therapists, acupuncturists, and of course, my PCA. They are all wonderful people. I am incredibly lucky to have them taking such good care of me—especially Pittsma. Nonetheless, I get very little privacy, and I find it difficult to speak my thoughts while people come and go. I'm not complaining, just explaining.

At this point, it's difficult to remember how dreadful I was feeling before my surgery. I am so much better now. The pressure sores on my feet are entirely healed, and I have even put on some weight. In fact, I feel better than I have in a long time. I am more myself.

And I realize that for me, right now in my life, this is as good as it is going to get, which leads me to reflect on something I said to Scott the week before my surgery. I was feeling especially down and told him that if anything went wrong during the surgery, he was to let me go. I notified my medical team and had the decision added to my record. When the surgeon came in to see me in the hospital prior to surgery, she asked me to confirm it.

Now, two months later, experiencing the benefits of good nutrition and a successful antidepressant, I ask myself if I still feel the same way. The answer is yes, not because I am feeling distressed or overburdened or overwhelmed. Quite the opposite. I am feeling positive and, at times, even buoyant. So this really seems like the optimal time to look at the future and make some decisions.

There are two treatments for ALS that are invasive. One is the G-tube, something I am very happy I agreed to. The other is a ventilation tube, to take over when my own ability to breathe fails. I have had ALS now for six years. I have a pretty good sense of how the disease is progressing. I believe that by the time I would need a ventilator, the rest of my body will have already shut down. So I have decided against a ventilator and have put this decision in writing, so there will be no mistakes. I feel extremely peaceful and content with this decision.

In a way, I feel that now I can get on with my life, a new aspect of which is something they are calling "recreational eating." I thought I already knew all about eating as recreation. It was to this consummate ability that I attributed what used to be my middle-age spread, now gone. But my new life with the G-tube gives "recreational eating" new meaning. For the first few weeks after my surgery, I was fed every two hours during the day. This meant that someone had to stop what they were doing—shoot, I had to stop when I was doing—so that a can of formula could be administered through the tube. As you can imagine, this got boring very quickly. Fortunately, an alternative was readily available. Using a cute little pump, formula can be administered through the tube overnight as I sleep. From the first night, it worked flawlessly. So now, when I get up in the morning, I have already consumed my basic nutrition for the day and can freely engage in—and truly relish—any other food I would like to take by mouth during the day. I can eat as little or as much as I like, when I like. The wonder of it is that the food I decide to eat tastes divine. So I nibble all day long and find it, well, *recreational.*

Scott is home at the moment, after trips to Texas and Wyoming for most of the month of June. No trips to Iraq are currently planned, but I'm told that could change. So we continue to look for more stable care alternatives. For now, I have the wonderful Pittsma on weekdays. She is truly a godsend.

As a result of the generosity of everyone who contributed to the party last weekend, we now have a small fund to hire someone to be with me in the evenings. So the process of locating such a person has begun. So once again, many thanks to all of you.

This week, as I have been falling asleep at night (lulled by the sweet music of the BiPAp, the G-tube pump, and the rhythmic snoring of my ancient dog), I see myself back in Tom and Diane's living room the way we were at the party last Sunday. The memory fills me with immense calm and well-being. In that gentle embrace, I drift happily off to sleep.

All my love,
Catherine

12 August 2007

Dear Ones,

Summer lethargy. It's the only thing that can account for my total lack of desire to be sitting in front of the computer. It's been a beautiful summer, and I have been fortunate to be able to spend a great deal of it out on my deck or front porch. I'm even reading trashy novels, just as if I were at the beach.

I have also had the pleasure of seeing all three of my siblings. They live so far away (Iowa, Oregon, and North Carolina) that it is indeed special when we can give each other a real hug.

Despite my laziness, things have been happening. Physically, my body continues on its course, ably supported by the various technologies that are now part of my daily life. I continue to be gratified and awed by the simplicity and efficiency of my feeding tube. But my right hand has now become very weak. I sometimes need help brushing my teeth and putting on my glasses. Thankfully, Pittsma is still with me, making my days delightful and easy.

For the short term, Pittsma will continue to be here for 40 hours a week. Thanks to the generosity of everyone who contributed to my party last month, I have also been able to hire someone to put me to bed at night. She can't begin for another week, and I'm hoping that she will also be able to fill in for Pittsma whose nursing classes begin in three weeks. Despite her classes, Pittsma plans to still be able to give me 24 hours each week.

I'm rather consumed by these kinds of details at the moment, since I can no longer be left alone, and I need skilled people taking care of me. This all raises a very important question. I liken it to Mohammed and the mountain. At the moment, the mountain is coming to Mohammed. I spend a lot of time advertising and interviewing caregivers. I hired two separate PCA's, at two separate times this summer. Both had seemed enthusiastic, but on their first day of work, neither of them called or showed up. I never saw them again. I've heard others describe similar experiences. So, this leaves me feeling wary and vulnerable. Pittsma has been a dream come true. I am hoping the woman I have just hired will be as wonderful.

But I am anxious, particularly because we have just learned that in two weeks Scott will be returning to Iraq for two months. Knowing that he would probably leave sooner or later, earlier this summer I began to question my paradigm: What would it look like if Mohammed went to the mountain?

So let me tell you about The Boston Home. It is a skilled nursing facility about a mile from my house. It was established over a hundred years ago to specifically meet the needs of people with neuromuscular diseases. At the suggestion of a friend, I actually toured this facility three years ago. At that time I was in a healthy state of denial. The facility looked nice, but I could never imagine myself needing it.

Last month, with Scott, I gave it another look. The Boston Home describes itself as a residential community. People who live there, primarily people with multiple sclerosis, often do so for 30 to 40 years. A good number of them are younger than I am. It is a big, sunny, well-run facility. In order to even be considered for their waiting list, which is quite long, one has to be vetted. So we spent four hours there on July 11, being interviewed and interviewing them. I felt like I had forgotten to take my SATs!

They have a two-part process. After the interview, they determine whether you would be a good fit for their community. If they feel you would be, then, and only then, are you placed on their waiting list. At this point, I am waiting to hear the results of step one.

The night before the interview, I was filled with misgivings. While it makes complete sense to think positively about going to where the care is, nonetheless it means leaving my home. And what if I didn't like it there? What if I went for my interview and came away with palpable dread? What if Scott hated it?

I am relieved that none of this happened. I like the facility very much. It seems like a genuine community. I spoke with a couple of residents who were very enthusiastic. Would it be like living at home? No. I would be well cared for, but it is an institution. There's no question about that. I would have a roommate and nowhere near the privacy I enjoy now. But I would be relieved of the burden of finding and keeping caregivers and I would also be lifting some of the anxiety that my family and friends are currently enduring on my behalf.

As one friend said to me recently: "Catherine, I always knew you would end up in an ashram!"

He's right. It feels a bit like that to me, too. While it is not a "spiritual community," they do have a spiritual director and a very definite leaning toward religion and spirituality. I even allowed myself to think about the prospect of moving there during my prime daily fretting time—just before I go to sleep at night. I had anticipated that allowing these thoughts to fill my head would cause anxiety, followed by sleeplessness. Instead, I found the prospect comforting. I slept soundly. So there you are.

It is distinctly possible that I may never be invited to move to The Boston Home. They may decide that I am not the right fit. And even if they decide otherwise and I am put on the waiting list, it could be months, even years, before they have an opening. So this is very far from a done deal.

In the meantime, in the midst of the flow of my wonderful daily and weekly visitors, I had a very special visitor. Dr. Joshi made a house call. He, his wife Shalmali, their daughter, and my friend Kathy, who introduced me to Dr. Joshi in the beginning, came to spend a rainy afternoon with me. After a little socializing, he and I repaired to the kitchen where we talked about my condition. He read my pulses and we shared current details of our spiritual lives. At the end of our visit, the rain came down so heavily we had to stop and watch it. It looked like an Indian monsoon.

Dr. Joshi has always been very honest with me, which is why I love and value him so much. On this visit, he noticed a change. Previously, he has always remarked on how strong my life force, or *prana*, is.

This time he said: "For the first time, I can feel your prana weakening."

I was not surprised to hear this, as I have been sensing it myself. It's not that I'm going to die in a week or month or even a year. It's just that, in some strange way, my body has finally realized it is sick. As always, I thanked Dr. Joshi for being candid. He prescribed an herb to help augment my energy. My energy doesn't actually feel that low, certainly not as intensely challenged as it was before my surgery. But I can feel myself slowing down. I would do very well south of the border now. *Mañana, mañana* . . . Can those of you who know me well believe this?

I hope you all are enjoying the remaining summer beauty.

All my love,
Catherine

25 October 2007

Dear Ones,

When Owen was very little, he used to take me for walks. He would lead; I would follow. Some days we made it to the end of the block. Some days we made it all the way around the block. On these walks, Owen often would suddenly squat down to look more closely at something on the ground. Then, if he deemed it worthy, he would stick it in his pocket. It was always hard for me to find the common thread in his collection of bolts, torn lottery scratch tickets, pull tabs to tin cans, and other less identifiable items. Finally one day, I asked him what he was collecting. With the absolute clarity of a four-year-old, he enlightened me:

"Mom, they are clues to the universe."

From then on, they were simply referred to as "clues." I never fully understood the connections he saw in what appeared to be detritus, but he did get me wondering about the apparent randomness of my own life. It was then that I stopped believing in coincidences and started looking for clues of my own.

It was in this frame of mind that I experienced two recent events. At the time, they seemed unexpected and unprovoked. Only later did I appreciate the messages each embodied.

The first happened three weeks ago. A punk kid put a rock through my front window. Nothing personal. I know that. He was just throwing a rock and got unlucky.

Galen asked, "Did you catch him?"

For a moment I imagined myself putting my wheelchair into hyper-drive, blasting after the miscreant, and whacking him upside the head. However, a quite different scene unfolded, one that had become a little too common of late. I—always so calm and unflappable—completely fell apart. I was overwhelmed with helpless frustration.

And yet I was not alone. Pittsma was with me, and shortly thereafter she was joined by my friend Sarah. The police were called. Neighbors were canvassed. Everyone gathered round. No real harm had been done, nothing irreparable, anyway. And contrary to assumptions about Dorchester, this is *not* a common occurrence here. So why did this happen?

The incident presented an opportunity to witness my own thinking process. Scott has been in Iraq now for five weeks. Whenever he goes away, I feel more fragile, less sure of myself—actually less myself. The rock through the window taught me that even in Scott's absence I am not alone. I am nowhere near as vulnerable as I may think.

The second event happened about a week later. I was sitting in the kitchen after dinner with a few friends when the phone rang. A voice at the other end asked if I was the Catherine Royce who wrote the NPR essay. He informed me that he was calling from the "Dr. Phil Show." They were planning a show marking the 10th anniversary of the publication of *Tuesdays with Morrie,* and they wanted someone currently living with ALS to appear on the show. Would I be interested? I was a bit incredulous at first, but played along.

Sure enough, he was a producer for "Dr. Phil," and we had a lengthy and delightful conversation. He asked me if I had read the popular book. When I told him I had not, he did not seem put out. The only hitch came when he asked if I could travel to LA. I told him it was doubtful, especially as the idea was for me to fly out on Tuesday, do the show on Wednesday, and fly home on Thursday. He said, however, that this would not be a problem. They would simply set me up with a web cam here at home. He said he would call back the next day to confirm.

Two days later he called to explain that they had found a woman in LA who could come into the studio. I later learned that she sits on the board of the ALS Association of Los Angeles and has had ALS a shorter time than I have. In the end, I was relieved. I have never seen "Dr. Phil," but could imagine that an appearance on his show would prolong my 15 minutes of fame. I'm happy to let someone else have their turn.

So, what was the point of this odd blip? Like the rock through the window, it helped me realize something important about my life. In my conversation with the producer, he referred to an interview I gave a few months ago in which I had stated that I would not wish to return to my pre-ALS existence, because living with ALS has taught me so much and has added richness to my life. Surrounded by a large community of friends, I have learned lessons about the giving and receiving of love that I might otherwise have missed.

Reviewing the phone conversation later, I realized that my life has really not changed all that much. The wealth of human interaction that has always been an integral part of my life remains undiminished. If anything, it has increased. My house has always been a place people came to. We used to joke that the reason burglars seemed to skip our house was because there was always someone home. This is more true now than ever, and I would not have it any other way.

These two insights came together nicely a couple of weeks ago. But it occurred to me that with so many different people taking care of me, there might be chaos in an emergency. I could imagine a frightened caregiver dialing 911, and some well-meaning EMT rushing to save my life. Definitely a worst-case scenario.

So one evening, I asked the Four Fabulous Females to meet with me. I asked each of them to tell me what she believed my wishes were. Each gave me a slightly different answer. Not good. I knew then that if I had failed to give those closest to me a clear message, it would be even more confusing for others. We agreed that a meeting with my ALS nurse practitioner was in order. He agreed to come to my house the following Monday.

Out of that meeting came a decision to transfer my care to the hospice team. This is in no way as dire as it sounds. I qualify for hospice because my breathing rate has dropped below a certain threshold. It does not mean my departure is imminent—not by a long shot. What it *does* mean is a kind of one-stop shopping. The hospice team knows my wishes. If there is an emergency, the first call is to the hospice team. They will direct everything else. This gives peace of mind to me and to all the wonderful people who care for me. So far, it has changed my life in very small ways, all of them good.

Being in hospice did give me one little scare. One member of the hospice team has the role of providing spiritual support. He called a couple of weeks ago and asked if he could come over. I was a little nervous but said okay. A couple of hours later he was coming through my gate holding what looked like a Bible.

"Oh, no," I thought. "I am so screwed."

I thought I had been sent a Christian Bible thumper. I have great reverence for Jesus Christ as a teacher; but I do not consider myself a Christian. So I thought this meeting would be at best, short—at most, painful.

How wrong could I be? A former Jesuit priest, he could not have been more perfect for who I am and where I am in my spiritual development. One of the first things he said to me was that he believes that he and God are one and the purpose of a human life is to fully realize this connection. How cool is that? When he left, I felt genuinely comforted. I will see him every week or so. What an incredible gift!

And speaking of gifts, some of you have begun receiving thank you notes from me. My sister Amanda came from Iowa and set up a template on my computer that enables me to write notes. The fact that I have been unable to personally and individually acknowledge the extraordinary generosity that I experienced in July has weighed heavily on me. I am delighted to finally be able to speak to each of you from my heart. If you haven't received a note yet, hang in there. You will. My new nighttime PCA, Sandra, has been working with me. She is wonderful and incredibly patient. So the notes actually come from Amanda, Sandra, me, and whoever takes them to the mailbox.

Otherwise, life has been quiet and enjoyable. The PCA makeup of my days changes from time to time. I had a rather bizarre encounter with a PCA last month. She was a born-again Christian who spent four very long days preaching, praying over me (and demanding that I pray with her), and loudly singing hymns. She was a character, or as my grandmother would have said: "She was a card, that should be dealt with." I've learned to be more selective about whom I hire. My stories about her made everyone laugh so hard that now whenever anything goes wrong, we blame her. She threw the rock through the window. She sent me two bad movies in a row from Netflix. But for her, the Red Sox would have won those early games in the Pennant playoffs. You catch my drift.

It has taken me a while to get around to writing this update. The weather has been spectacular, and I find myself irresistibly drawn to sitting in the sun on my front porch and watching the wind blow through the leaves as they change color and then fall. Also, there has been the little matter of the Red Sox. The first World Series game was last night. My hair just gets grayer and grayer. It's a good thing I can no longer bite my nails.

Otherwise, the news from the Boston Home is that I am number one on the waiting list. They could call tomorrow, next week, next year, or whenever; but things at home now are great, so, no hurry. Scott should be home in a couple of weeks. He is currently in Tikrit. More when he returns.

All my love,
Catherine

20 November 2007

Dear Ones,

Scott has just returned from two months in Iraq, to what he refers to as a "home invasion." Until he pointed it out to me, I had not realized how much our house has become a bit of a three-ring circus, particularly since I went on hospice (Yes, that's what it's called. One is "on hospice"). There are so many people taking care of me now, and—lucky me—they are all wonderful.

Depending on the day of the week, my morning begins with either Pittsma or Ursula. I have described Pittsma before—young, energetic, funny, and a source of endless teasing. Ursula is slightly older than I am. She's from Trinidad and speaks with a pleasing lilt. She has a wicked sense of humor—very dry. She is very strong, and can move me around like a sack of potatoes. She is also very bossy. Fortunately, so am I. My daytime crew is augmented, Monday through Friday, by a support team of visiting nurse, home health aide, chaplain, acupuncturist, psychotherapist, and hairstylist. Which one of these could I possibly live without? None, obviously.

My home health aide Vivianne is, like Pittsma, originally from Haiti. When Vivianne and Pittsma get together, I get a shower and about an hour's worth of laugh therapy. I call them the Haitian Sisterhood. Pittsma teases Vivianne, in English and in Creole. Vivianne waits patiently, often twirling a pair of my underpants around her wrist like a hula hoop, for Pittsma to finish with me, so Vivianne can get me dressed. They often forget that I speak a little French, and Haitian Creole is enough like French that I can frequently understand them when they get going. This is a source of more hilarity.

When the sun goes down, there is a change of guard. Pittsma or Ursula goes home, and Sandra arrives. After the day's boisterous activity, Sandra is a beacon of peace and calm—the perfect end to my day. Her presence is soothing and tranquil. As I am writing this, it is evening. She and I are here alone. The house is quiet. The only break in this serenity is the loud, unpredictable, manic barking of our increasingly eccentric dog.

Then, sometime between 9:00 and 10:00, an overnight buddy arrives, one of a small group of family and friends. She or he (usually she) spends the night upstairs, cuddled up with my baby monitor. If I need help during the night, these are my angels. One brings her dog with her. I woke up one night just in time to see a black form race jubilantly through my room, followed closely by another form, in a more frantic mode. I sleep with a full face mask, so laughing while wearing this mask sounds like strangling. There are many sounds—the BiPAp, the feeding pump, my breathing, the dog snoring—that my sleepover buddies have to contend with every night. God bless them.

A three-ring circus, you say? Home invasion? And I haven't even mentioned the people who bring us dinners. Remember when I was such a private person? Well, the other day, when I found myself carrying on a full conversation while sitting on the toilet, I knew I had crossed some sort of line. This morning, Scott and I made a grocery list while Vivianne gave me a shower. I am amazed to discover how many people I now meet for the first time while I am in some state of partial or complete nudity. It's just the way it is.

Sages of many faiths often comment on our relationships with our bodies. Most major religions have sects that renounce the flesh in order to achieve spiritual enlightenment. As you might have noticed, I am not one of these. I have always rather liked the flesh, but am renouncing it nonetheless—or perhaps it is renouncing me. I often imagine that God carries a chisel and everyday uses this tool to lob off some part of my physical self that I no longer need. Certainly, if someone had told me even three years ago that I would welcome and even delight in the constant presence of others in the most intimate aspects of my life, I would have been incredulous. Now, it simply feels commonplace—hardly worth mentioning.

One might even go so far as to say that ALS is critical to my path to realization. As I become more and more dependent on others to get me through the day, much of what I thought of as critical to my sense of self is being stripped away. Amazingly, I'm not missing much of it. I am sure this is because I am in a very special place. Despite everything that is happening to me, and maybe even because of it, I am surrounded by love and caring to a degree beyond my imagination.

This sense of something being beyond my imagination has always been a hallmark for me of divine presence. People often say you can be anything you can imagine, yet I've always found this comment frustrating. I would think: "But my imagination is so pathetically limited!" Thankfully, I am not constrained in this way anymore. Everything that is happening to me now is truly beyond my imagination. This is a gift.

A friend, Bindu Holder, has created a beautiful painting of a Shiva Nataraj. She gave me a reproduction of this painting for my birthday last week. I think I will take it with me.

I think I will take it with me. That sentence punctuates my days. Last week, I received an e-mail from The Boston Home telling me that they have "an opening pending." So, it looks like I will be busting a move sooner rather than later. I will keep you informed.

I wish you all a truly thankful Thanksgiving.

All my love,
Catherine

27 November 2007

Dear Ones,

And now the news we have all been waiting for—or that I have
been waiting for. (I am still the center of everyone's universe, am I
not?) This is one of those good news—bad news scenarios.

I always like getting the bad news out of the way first. So here it is: As
of Wednesday, November 28, I will no longer be living at 1 Larchmont
St. For the past 30 years, this has been my home; my attachment
to it is umbilical. Most of the important events and the cherished
memories of my adult life happened here. More significantly, after
34 years, Scott and I will no longer be living under the same roof.
This makes my heart ache and my eyes fill with tears.

On with the good news: As of Wednesday, November 28, I will
be living at The Boston Home. I have already told you some details
about this wonderful place. For more, you can check out their web
site at *www.thebostonhome.org.* At the moment, I am filled with anxiety
at the prospect of this change. But I know, beyond a shadow of doubt,
that this is the right move. I will be cared for in a way that cannot
possibly be duplicated here in my home. This alone will significantly

relieve stress all around—for me, Scott, Owen and Galen, and for that magnificent circle of friends and family who have been so generous with their love and caring. Fortunately, The Boston Home is less than a mile from 1 Larchmont St. I can visit whenever I like. And all those who have been keeping me such dear company can continue to do so. I am free to come and go as I please and others are welcome to do the same.

I am delighted to discover that, even at this stage of my illness and my life, I can still entertain new adventures. Truly, this is much more good news than bad. A moment ago, I was tearful, but that has passed. Of course, I will continue to stay in touch. There will be much to learn and much to share.

Big adventure. Huge change. And I thought going to India was a big deal!

All my love,
Catherine

Part Five

17 January 2008

Dear Ones,

And we're back. Six weeks of cyber silence—this I had not factored into my mental preparations for moving to The Boston Home. But that's how long it took Verizon to hook up my internet cable here in my cozy little room. About a week after I moved here, I began composing an update that began: "Oh, my God! Oh, my God! Oh, my God! What have I done? Oh, my God! Oh, my God! Oh, my God! Bedpans! Oh, my God! Oh, my God! Oh, my God! Diapers! Oh, my God! Oh, my God! Oh, my God! Roommate! Oh, my God! Oh, my God! Oh, my God! Strangers! Oh, my God! Oh, my God! Oh, my God! And don't even get me started on the food!"

The first couple of weeks were really exclamation points. A photograph would have shown my eyes bugging out of my head, respiration shallow. The last time I had to adjust to such a major life change was after my first child was born. Nothing less than stepping into an utterly new world. When the Director of Admissions saw me on day three, she remarked: "Big changes. I bet you didn't know you had it in you." I shot back, "Actually, it never occurred to me

I didn't have it in me." My ego was piqued. Of course I have it in me!

Six weeks later, we—The Boston Home and I—are adjusting to each other quite nicely. Everyone here is extremely kind and willing to help me in any way. They hate it when I cry. Well, let's be honest, *I* hate it when I cry, so immediately we had something in common. And in those first few weeks, I did a bit of crying, I'll admit. I'm not even ashamed of it. Now that's a change!

What is it about this disease that seems to be all about my processes of elimination? I haven't changed that much in three years. I'm still a WASP. I still don't shit. And if I do, it doesn't smell and, no matter what, I don't talk about it. Nonetheless, here I am, once again, dwelling on things that have nothing to do with me, if you catch my meaning. However, you cannot have missed the dreaded words "bedpan" and "diaper" above. Can these words really be related to my life? Apparently, they can. I will spare you the details (Shoot, I'd spare myself the detail!). Suffice it to say, big change, big, big change—but not often enough.

The Boston Home lives up to its reputation. There is an enormous emphasis here on community. When I arrived, I was immediately assigned a buddy. She, Mary Jo, has been my lifeline as I make my way through the complexities of this new life. For example, it was she who explained to me the division of labor. We have nurses and certified nursing assistants. The former dispense medications, give cough assist treatments, and hook me up to my feeding pump at night. The latter take care of everything related to the preceding paragraph. They also bathe me, put me to bed, get me out of bed, dress me, brush my teeth, help me with my various headsets (telephone and computer), pick up the many things I have a talent for dropping all day long, and feed me. One fails to understand this division of labor at one's peril. I had never before realized how long it can take to get your teeth brushed if you ask the wrong person.

The building is large and completely barrier free. Even now in the depths of winter, I can cruise around, see new sights, get a breath of fresh air, and be sociable, as I wish. I have many more options for making mischief than I had at home since I started using a wheelchair. There was really no way for me to anticipate how much change this move would create. (*Change.* Aren't there a bunch of politicians running around using this word a lot right now? They have *no* idea!) What I underestimated most was how much advocacy I would have to do on my own behalf because there are significant differences between ALS and MS. The four major differences that I've encountered so far are: I will never be incontinent; I will never lose sensation in my body; my breathing issues are more urgent because of the increasing weakness in my diaphragm; and finally, I will die of ALS (unless I get hit by a bus first). ALS is a terminal illness; technically speaking, MS is not. In practical terms, this means that the whole bedpans and diapers thing is inappropriate for me. It also means that I feel pain, and that pain relief, whether in the form of medication or laying on of hands, is critical for me. And finally, it means that when I ring my call button because I'm choking, I need help NOW.

To their credit, the staff has been open and more than willing to make the necessary adjustments. It has meant, however, that I have spent the last six weeks educating each and every person who works with me. It's required patience I didn't know I had. But in the end, it's in my best interest and, as an added benefit, it has allowed me to get up close and personal with a wonderful new group of people very quickly.

As always, the thing that has maintained my sanity and good humor has been the steady stream of visitors, family and friends, many of them bearing edible food. Okay, I exaggerate. The food here is edible. I am just very spoiled and therefore exceedingly grateful that I am not dependent upon this food to keep me alive. "Recreational eating" has taken on a whole new meaning.

As I write, I find it a challenge to give a full picture of my new life. Sharing a story or two is probably the best approach.

Story number one: The other night Scott came to visit, and I accompanied him to the front door when he left. This included an elevator ride to the ground floor. I live on the first floor. I said goodnight to Scott and headed back to the elevator, where I encountered one of my sister residents struggling to make her way onto the elevator. She can no longer use her hands, so she employs her chin to drive her wheelchair, and the mechanism is not working properly.

In a barely audible voice, she asks me to hold the door open so she can make her way into the car. I do as she asks, and after a little struggle, she finally makes it onto the elevator. As she enters the car, I back up to make room. The doors close, and we ascend to the first-floor. The doors open, and my companion attempts to back up, so I can exit. Instead, her chair shoots forward, pinning me in the back of the car. The doors close. The elevator ascends to the second-floor. The doors open, and again my companion attempts to back up. Again, she shoots forward. Now not only can I not move, I also cannot reach any of the emergency buttons. The doors close. The elevator descends to the first-floor. The doors open.

"Help, help!" I yell.

The doors close. My companion begins to silently weep. The elevator descends to the ground floor. The doors open.

"Help, help!"

The doors close. The elevator ascends to the first-floor. The doors open.

"Help, help!" I hear voices.

The doors close. The elevator ascends to the second-floor. My companion continues to weep. The doors open.

"Help, help!" The doors close. The elevator descends to the first-floor. The doors open. There, standing in the open doorway, her hands on her hips, is the head of nursing. Helen is a solidly built woman with a wicked sense of humor. "Are you having fun?" she asks. I laugh. She wades into the car and manually extracts my companion, who is no longer weeping. I exit the elevator. Helen pats me on the shoulder as I wheel by.

Story number two: During my first week, I left my room just as the local curmudgeon—an essential character for any viable community—wheeled by. A nurse, standing in the hallway, asked him if he had met me.

"No!" he growled.

"Well, this is Catherine. She used to be a dancer," explained the nurse.

"Were you a stripper?" he responded.

To get the full benefit of his question, you have to hear it in the full bloom of his Boston accent: "Wuh you a strippah?" This is my new life. It isn't ever boring. More tales of new life to follow.

All my love,
Catherine

30 April 2008

Dear Ones,

So l-o-o-o-ng.

To recount for you all that has transpired in the past five months (I can't believe it has actually been five months!) feels somewhat daunting. But let me begin with the reassurance that I am doing well. The decision to move into The Boston Home remains a very right and gratifying one. I am well cared for by sweet and loving people, and after a five-month ordeal with the state of Massachusetts, my continuing here is finally financially assured.

Physically, my body continues to weaken. I now struggle to hold up my head and my breathing has become much more labored. However, thanks to the brilliance of the staff here, a BiPAP has been mounted on the back of my wheelchair. So I have ongoing access to breathing support. I don't use it all the time, but it's nice to know it's there. Pain is also now under control. After some trial and error, we've come up with the right combination of medications to keep me comfortable. Breathing support, no pain, loving care. It's a very good deal!

I had an image the other day of a boat, really just a dinghy. It was tied to the shore by a multitude of lines. But as I was watching it, the lines, one by one, came loose and dropped into the water. As each line disconnected, the dinghy rocked gently in the water and began to move away from the shore. Soon, it was only connected by one or two lines. And this is where my image ended. This is where I feel I am. I am a dinghy, weather worn, open, simple, utilitarian. Slowly but surely the lines to my life as I have known it are dropping away. Curiously, the dinghy in my image had no oars.

Perhaps the most profound line to fall away has been my relationship with Scott. I moved out of our home of 30 years, and our marriage contract changed. It was wrenching, and at the time, I thought, my heart would break. But it didn't. I think, in fact, hearts do not break. They just experience pain and either expand or contract. My heart expanded. By moving here, I have been invited to experience the true nature of unconditional love. It is the kind of love that Scott and I promised each other when we got married. In our vows, we promise not to "honor and obey" but rather to be each other's "beloved and friend." Over 33 years of marriage, we added other labels to "beloved and friend:" wife, husband, parent, home owner. Suddenly, with my move here, all those labels fell away. What remained is what we started out with, what we promised each other: beloved and friend.

This past year has been filled with the pain of physical and psychological separation. But in the end, our spiritual union remains strong and blessed. Scott is here with me for several hours every day that work allows. He probably will be returning to Iraq sometime in July, but since the first of the year he has mostly been here; and we have made the most of our time together.

Another line that has come undone is the loss of my dear mother-in-law. Jane Marie Garbutt Nagel Skillman was a great woman, perfect mother-in-law, and spectacular grandmother. Her love for me was unconditional. Her love for her grandchildren was ecstatic. Her daughter described her as "a continent." She was a public health nurse in California during a remarkable time in its history. When she learned that Scott and I were determined to live on the East Coast, she announced that that would be all right as long as she could have her grandchildren for a month every year; Scott and I were not invited. She took them on such adventurers: a dude ranch, floating down the Sacramento River on a houseboat, Disneyland. I feel her absence keenly.

I am not looking forward to Scott's being away, but as I look around me here at The Boston Home, I see how truly blessed I am. There are many residents here who never receive a single visitor, while I am teased mercilessly by the staff if a day goes by when I do *not* have a visitor. I joke that 2049 Dorchester Avenue is actually 1 Larchmont St-B. Everyone seems to have moved the 1 Larchmont St. operation over here in an almost seamless fashion.

My days are full. Because I am on hospice, a woman of boundless energy and good cheer named Clotilda starts almost every day with me. She bathes me, dresses me, brushes my teeth, combs my hair, puts on a little makeup, and hands me a cup of tea. She has far better taste in clothing that I do, so I leave all those decisions up to her. In fact, the other nurses aides say they can discern when Clotilda is not here by what I'm wearing.

After Clotilda leaves, and after a nurse has coaxed large globs of applesauce riddled with colorful little pills down me, I have a weekly schedule that includes a reading group, a writing group, a newcomer's group (a.k.a. Let Me Tell You What's Bugging Me Today), and a meditation group. In between, there are delicious periods of napping, reading, and just gazing quietly out the window. The Boston Home has its own little campus. There are times when I look out the window and I forget I'm in Dorchester. At the moment, the gardens are resplendent with flowering trees, daffodils, and tulips. On warm days, I can go outdoors. But I came here at the end of November and don't know much about the garden yet. At the end of my corridor, there is a large solarium. It looks out over the garden and the surrounding neighborhood. I spend a good portion of every day in this room. It's also where I sit with friends, both friends I live with here and friends who visit.

The friends who visit continue to keep me feeling loved and connected to the world. Since I moved, they have become more of a lifeline than ever. My transition from home to the Boston Home—"Home home" as I call it—has not been without drama. There have been tears and anger, misunderstandings and fear. But I have never been alone, even when it seemed that way. In fact, one tearful evening I found myself laughing at myself as I told an aide who was trying to console me that I would "phone a friend"—just like the game shows.

And then there are the friends I have made here at Home home. If you think *I* have a tale to tell, you ain't heard *nothin'*. Here, I am one of many. Not everyone can tell their story, but the ones who can, are an inspiration to me. In fact, I am currently helping a high school student who is compiling a series of profiles of various residents. Their stories convey much more about my life here. I won't use their real names.

I am on my second roommate, an eventuality I had not anticipated. I think of myself as being pretty adaptable. I figured I'd move in with a roommate and we'd live happily ever after, but I learned otherwise. My first roommate was an eccentric artist whose illness has accentuated some extreme aspects of her personality. Our rooms here are set up so that the beds are foot to foot, with a small passage in between. So basically, when we are in the room and our curtains are not drawn (I find it claustrophobic when the curtains are drawn), we end up staring into each other's space. My first roommate's space was dominated by a self-portrait that loomed large over the room. Let's just say I got to a point where I could no longer look at that painting.

My new roommate is a delight. She speaks with difficulty, but we have found ways to communicate and enjoy each other's company. My family and friends have also become fond of her. The room is filled with plants and flowers. On any given afternoon, you will find the two of us napping while she allegedly watches the soaps. At first, people would come in and try to talk with us during this sacred time, but now we are left alone.

Speaking of sacred time, three afternoons a week I lead the community meditation. I am used to meditation sessions being fairly staid affairs. Not here. Sometimes, I meditate alone; sometimes with staff members; most often with one to seven other residents. We freely acknowledge that some of the residents regard our sessions as a sort of supervised nap, complete with snoring.

The other day I arrived to find Judy already in the room. I asked her if she had come to meditate. She nodded her head. We waited a few minutes for others to arrive.

Suddenly she asked me, "Are you here for the two o'clock meeting?"

I answered, "No, I am here for the three o'clock meditation. Would you like to join me?"

"Yes," she said, "I have been meditating for the past 10 years."

I love meditating and especially in the company of other long time meditators. So I was delighted by her company, and, as no one else had arrived, I led the two of us into meditation. We had been sitting in silence together for about five minutes—it's usually a 20 minute meditation—when Judy suddenly turned on her wheelchair, which makes a beeping noise, and headed out of the room, thanking me as she left. I was reminded that it's always important to know when your meditation is over. Mine continued for another 15 minutes.

We have a resident here whom I will call Jack. He hosts his own gathering every evening after dinner. His sessions have a faithful following. I would be fortunate to have such a regular group for meditation! His gathering even has a name. It's called simply "Jokes." Jack reads jokes. He has a sort of WC Fields delivery, very dry. He'll read any joke he finds anywhere—no matter how raunchy, no matter how un-PC, no matter how sexist. He only seems to draw the line at race jokes. He doesn't care if you laugh or not. As a result, people do laugh, sometimes uproariously. He also encourages audience participation.

For example, most of his jokes have a title. He will read the title and, invariably, someone in the audience will echo him.

Jack: "The penguin and the state trooper."

Audience member: "The penguin and the state trooper."

Jack: "A blonde walks into a bar."

Audience member: "A blonde walks into a bar."

Also there is mandatory participation for any joke that begins with "The (noun) was so big . . ."—"How big was it?" or "Knock,

knock . . ." In fact, if Jack thinks you're snoozing, he'll call on you to anticipate the punchline.

Every night except Wednesday. I don't know how he does it and, frankly, I don't know why it's so funny. It just is. Scott and my sister Becket have visited these sessions, so it's not just me.

And what do I do in Wednesday night? I have a standing date with Ted, who told me I should use his real name. We watch the news together.

Most days, I am delighted by the unexpected.

A few days ago, it was unusually warm. At the back of the building, there is a beautiful garden complete with koi pond, flowers, bird feeders, Tibetan prayer flags, and various spots to sit quietly and enjoy the warmth. This garden, however, does not open until the first of May. Not so this year. There is a large double door leading into the garden. That day I happened to exit the elevator just in time to witness a resident ram his wheelchair into the door enough times to force the door to open. It was a little like opening the doors to the Bastille. Within minutes, the garden was filled with happy residents. There was a bit of administrative grumbling, but the garden is now officially open.

Shortly after arriving here, I was napping in my room and became aware that I was not alone. I opened my eyes to find one of my sister residents sitting silently opposite me.

"I love you," she said and then quietly wheeled herself out of the room.

Later, when I asked about her, I was told that she is exceptionally shy and her visit was unusual. She and I now have lunch together every day that she is well enough to come to the table. She is a bright spot in my day.

It gives me great pleasure to be writing to you again. I've had technical difficulties in the past few months that have served as a disincentive. I have also, to be honest, felt so overwhelmed that I just could not find the words. We'll see what happens next.

Thanks for being with me.

All my love,
Catherine

30 May 2008

Dear Ones,

This past weekend I had a glimpse of the future. It looks like a shiny, luminescent path of tiny smooth pebbles leading into a dark wood. The path is beguiling and frightening at the same time. As an aide was getting me ready for bed last Saturday night, I stopped breathing. There was no gasping for air, only the silence of an inhale not taken. She rolled me back over immediately and I was fine again.

Earlier in the week, I had visited my wonderful ALS team at Mass General. It's evident just from looking at me that most of my breathing is being done by superficial muscles in my chest and neck. This observation precipitated a discussion, once again, about my desires concerning artificial, permanent ventilation. And once again, I confirmed that I would prefer to allow my illness to take its course uninterrupted. This is not, however, a decision that I must make now. I can revisit the decision for the rest of my life and change my mind at any time.

However, I have turned a corner. And I am overwhelmed with gratitude for the way in which my family, friends, hospice workers, and the staff here turned the corner with me. I have been assured that I will be kept comfortable, and specifically *how* I will be kept comfortable, as my body weakens and breathing becomes more difficult. To that end, a meeting has been called to include everyone who supports me medically. By the end of the meeting, I and they will know what the course will look like. I now find that I need breathing assistance, with my BiPAP, almost nonstop. This is a kind of benchmark that indicates that I have 12 months (more or less) to continue sending updates.

It truly feels as though I am embarking on a charmed but frightening walk in a dark forest. The path is dazzling but the woods are frightening. I'm not so much afraid of dying as I am of the process of dying. Frankly, I'm scared.

But I am reminded again and again that this illness has been and continues to be a blessing. I asked to know myself as completely as possible, believing that by so doing I would draw closer to knowing God. There is nothing in this world so compelling to me as this intention. I feel this has happened and continues to happen. I've gotten my money's worth.

I also continue to believe that I am in the best possible place to complete this process. Before I moved here, I believed that when the end was near, I would want to go home. Now, I am content to stay put at "Home home." There is something very special about this place and I'm happy my life has brought me here. It is from Home home that I want to embark on the next step of my journey.

And besides, life never stands still. What else is new? I am learning a new language. A large proportion of the nursing staff here is Haitian. So, Haitian Creole slips into our daily conversations. My current favorite is not exactly a word, it's a sound: *OH-oh,* with the emphasis on the first *oh*. It can mean many things: *Whoops!, Look out!, Oh dear!, Incredible!,* to name a few. It's surprising how a new expression can ooze so easily into ones daily language. I think *OH-oh* at moments such as these:

"Housekeeping, please report to the first-floor nurse's station. Bring a mop."

"Supper tonight will be cream cheese and jelly on white bread."

"I'll be back," spoken, in the midst of putting me to bed or getting me up, by an aide who would never, ever catch herself saying "I'll be *right* back."

"Catherine, we'd like to experiment with a new kind of brief." (A "brief" is a euphemism for adult diaper. Let me assure you, there is absolutely, positively nothing brief about an adult diaper.)

"Mary would like to speak with you."

This last one requires explanation. Mary is Home home's social worker. She is beautiful, vivacious, kind, empathetic and, for all that, someone you would never want to cross. Being summoned to Mary's office can mean many things.

When I write these updates, I still feel that I am writing for the intimate group of friends I began with when I went to India. Even though I know there are a few more readers now, I am always startled when someone outside my original circle refers to something they read in an update.

You may recall from the last update that I was witness to an act of civil disobedience. It was a little matter of someone ramming down a garden door. So I was asked to come to Mary's office. Mary closed the door and pulled her chair up next to my chair. *OH-oh,*

"So, Catherine, we understand you know who broke down the garden door," says Mary.

My mind races madly to figure out how "we" found this out. But no time for that as Mary is continuing.

"We need to know who it is."

"On no! I promised him I wouldn't tell."

"Him?"

Oh God, I'm no good at this! Suddenly, I am aware of two things: The more I say, the more trouble I'm going to get into; and for the first time, I am seeing my updates as a liability. While I'm thinking and avoiding looking Mary in the eye, she continues.

"We have a couple of residents that we are working with on anger management. If it's any of these people, we really need to know."

The very first name on her list is our miscreant. What can I say? I caved. I gave him up. After leaving Mary's office, I felt I would be going back to homeroom where all the kids would know that I was a rat.

Finally, on another subject, I have told you how much I like my roommate. For our purposes, I will call her Gloria. Gloria can no longer speak clearly or move unassisted, but she does have some use of her hands and arms. The Boston Home is famous for its use of adaptive technologies. In Gloria's case, she has been provided with a talking box. It's a small box that sits in front of her. On the face of the box is an array of buttons; each button is aligned with a particular phrase or word. When Gloria presses a particular button, the box speaks that particular phrase or word. The most frequently used buttons are *yes* and *no*.

One quiet afternoon a few weeks ago, we were both in the room. Gloria indicated to me that she needed some help. She was in bed, so I rolled over to her and asked,

"Is this something I can do for you?"

Gloria is well aware of my physical limitations; the list of things I can do for her is short. Specifically, I can hand her the TV remote and her call button, and I can, sometimes, raise and lower the head of her bed. So that afternoon, her answer to my first question was *Yes.* I then proceeded down the list of things we knew I could do.

Hand her the TV remote? *Yes!* So I did that.

Hand her the call button? *Yes!* So I did that.

Raise or lower her bed? *No!*

"Gloria, is there anything else you need?" *Yes!*

"Is it something I can do for you?" *Yes!*

So I begin looking all around her bed and her room. I can't figure it out. What does she need to have done that I can do for her?

"Gloria, I'm stumped. I can't think of anything else. Are you sure this is something I can do for you?"

Yes!

So I look around some more. My eyes rest on a photograph of a young woman in African dress. It holds pride of place among Gloria's vast array of photographs. And then it comes to me.

"Gloria, would you like me to sit here with you and continue asking you questions?"

Yes!

And so began an amazing conversation in which I learned a great deal about Gloria's life and we, who had been living in the same room together for five months, were having our very first conversation.

Since then, we have become friends in a unique and deeply pleasing way.

So, from my current location on the luminous path in the dark wood, I will write again soon.

All my love,
Catherine

27 August 2008

Dear Ones,

Am I living in the middle of a mixed metaphor? Perhaps I am the last to notice. Well, there's the dinghy and then there's the luminescent path. I know that I am supposed to work with one metaphor at a time. Not this time. It would be like choosing between children. Or maybe I'm just being lazy. But as the country song goes: That's my story and I'm sticking to it.

I have wonderful news to share with you that both delights and saddens me. Two weeks ago, Galen left for England to begin her first year of medical school. This is something she has been wanting and working very hard toward for a number of years now, and I am so proud and happy for her. At the same time, I am not sure how I will manage without her. Ever since my diagnosis, she has been a source of strength and joy. Her unwavering support has been an incalculable blessing. But I *will* manage. I always do because, although Galen is irreplaceable, my life is full and I want for very little. In fact, I am quite spoiled. It's just that Galen spoiled me in a very special way. But how could I not be thrilled for her? She will make an extraordinary doctor.

In a way, Galen's moving along in her life, moves me along in mine. One more line disconnects from the shore and drops into the water. The dinghy bobs gently and moves a little further into deeper water. I experience this movement both as a source of contentment and excitement. This—here comes that mixed metaphor!—is the luminescent path I am on. The contentment appears as I sit in the garden here at Home home watching the birds squabble as they jockey for position in the water above the koi pond. Simply being in the garden on a beautiful day is a source of tremendous peace and well-being.

The excitement is something that has been growing on me. I noticed about a year ago, while I was still living at home, that the movement of wind through large trees was captivating. There was something about it that pulled my attention. Now I am surrounded by a campus endowed with a variety of mature trees, especially along the back of the property that abuts the garden. All during last winter, I would gaze at the naked skeletons of these beautiful trees. In the spring, after the trees had leafed out, we had several days of violent wind. I watched the leaves dancing in the wind. Each leaf moved according to its size and shape. The movement was intoxicating. I was swept away and in this moment came to understand my ultimate destiny. The energy that moved through those trees was the same energy that lives in me. When I die, that energy will be released and I will once again become one with this power and magnificence.

I have now learned a new Haitian Creole word. It's a marvelously descriptive word that moved quite effortlessly into my vocabulary. The word is *bunda*. When I go to bed at night, I have two pillows that we use to take pressure off my bunda. They are now known as my bunda pillows. Everyone here uses this word.

People have been asking me how my meditation group is going. I have discovered that a meditation session indoors on a beautiful day cannot compete with the beguiling call of the garden. I make the announcement for meditation, and no one comes. But then I go outside, and there they all are, quietly sitting in the garden. Most have their eyes closed. So I figure, anyone who is not snoring loudly, must be meditating. Right?

As many of you know, I have embarked on a new adventure. The thing I said I would never do, I am doing. Thanks to the clear vision and persistence of the spiritual director here at Home home, my letters to you are about to become a book. I always said that I did not have the energy both to write the letters and become involved in a book project, so I chose to write the letters. However, I also said that if anyone else wanted to pick up the book project, I would be delighted. That seemed like the moral equivalent of putting a $250,000 house on the market for over $1 million, not negotiable. And yet, it has happened. An entire garden of publishing professionals has sprung up around me: editors, artists, photographers, writers, and most of all, someone to move the entire project forward. We are self publishing and our goal is to have book in hand by Christmas.

Since all of my letters have been written to you, I think of the book as more your book than mine. Throughout the three years we have been meeting in this space, each letter has been a surprise and a joy to me. Every time I finish one, I assume it will be my last. I never intended to go on for so long. On the other hand, I never intended not to. Thus, every time I finish a letter, I think to myself: *Oh, good. That's the last time I have to do that.* And yet, almost as soon as I finish one letter, another begins to form in my mind. When composing the letter in my mind begins disrupting my sleep, I sit down and pour the words into this journal to my Dear Ones. Thank God you are there!

Until recently, the process of moving words from brain to laptop has been relatively effortless. You know how smitten I am with my voice recognition software. The key to happiness with voice recognition software, however, is the *voice*. Mine is leaving me. Therefore, a process that used to be almost easy has now become arduous. What this means for the future of these letters I'm not sure. But it's quite possible that this will be my last letter.

I could be wrong. You have probably noticed that my letters are fewer and farther between. So there may be more—I just don't know. But, for the first time since I started writing to you in 2005, I am finding the process of sharing my experience with you overwhelming.

So I will say what may be turn out to be a premature goodbye. You know the path I am on. I feel the urge to continue down the path more insistent every day. The things that used to pull on me, to get my attention, to distract me, no longer worry me. The only thing that still consistently captures my attention is love in its many forms: my family, my friends, the new friends I have made since moving to Home home, and beyond that, paying attention to and searching for love as it manifests all around me every day. My great teacher has said: "The heart is the hub of all sacred places. Go there and roam." It's a full time job.

I told a friend recently that I was contemplating writing my last letter to you. I was having trouble writing it—it seemed so final. So I told her I was going to write this letter and immediately follow it with another letter that simply said "Just kidding." It could happen.

In the meantime, let me go where my heart tells me to go. Let me say goodbye and thank you all for your attention and love. If there is more to tell you from the luminescent path, I will try to communicate it. It just may not be in this form.

Here is what my letters to you these past three and a half years have taught me. Wherever I am, whatever I am doing, whatever is happening to me, I'm fine.

Know that you are, and always will be, my Dear Ones.

All my love,
Catherine

ACKNOWLEDGEMENTS

Before this was a book, it was an adventure. I needed to go to India and thirty six people agreed. Thanks to their generosity, I found myself in Nagpur, India, in January 2005. I was there to receive treatment for ALS, my benefactors wanted regular updates on my experience. Overwhelmed by the prospect of sending multiple emails, one of the smartest young women I know, Caitlin Burbridge, created the perfect solution. Thus was born the website known as *www.sendcatherinetoindia.com*.

Thus, also, began a journey into gratitude. Looking back over my life, I might be tempted to see myself as an ungrateful wretch. I wasn't, but when the first contributions to my India trip arrived, I was at a loss to know how to properly and fully acknowledge the gift I had been given. Life's been a lot like that ever since. So to begin, I must, once again, thank my benefactors who made that trip possible.

Dr, Sunil Joshi and his loving treatment in Nagpur and later here in Boston established in me a sense of well being and health that I carry with me to this day. I have been graciously maintained in this state through the acupuncture skills of Barbara Parton.

On my return from India, I was embraced and held sacred by my husband, Scott Nagel and my children, Owen and Galen, They were the nucleus of an ever expanding circle of select friends who suddenly became intimate partners in my daily life. Primary among these are the 4 Fabs + 3: Sarah Bachrach, Jean Knox, Diane McCormack, Sheryl DiNisco, my dancing partner Inara DeLeon, my childhood friend Catharine Roehrig, and my baby sister Becket Royce McCough. Early on, it was their care that gave me the time, the focus and the fortitude to continue to write the letters that we referred to as "Updates." I am grateful to my sisters Becket and Amanda Royce Hale for the beautiful audio book. I thank my brother Tripp Royce for always being my brother.

Fairly shortly after my return from India, I lost the ability to type. Enter, voice recognition software—specifically Dragon Naturally Speaking. Without this miracle of modern science, the letters might have ended in 2005. But no . . .

In the early stages of writing the letters, I had incomparable support from my Hingham writers group: Eleanor Hughes, Marcia Cham, Jan Bacon, Carol Ertman, Virginia Pomeroy, and Rosemary Brennan. Support also came from the writing class at The Osher Lifelong Learning Institute at the University of Massachusetts, Boston, especially from the instructor, Carter Jefferson.

And then there came the day I met a small, unassuming Ursuline nun, Sr. Bridget Haase. In the process of blessing my hands and the work they do, she asked me if we could have a word. She told me she had been reading my website and she felt called to turn the content into a book. It is a simple but true statement: no nun, no book. And then, quite suddenly, the pieces all seemed to fall into place.

Led by the indomitable Jean Knox, whose organizing and culinary genius fed the author and the book in ways no one else could, and in collusion with sister editor extraodinaire, Christopher Corkery, my somewhat rambling letters took on a form of wholeness. Jean and Christopher were the early blooms in a garden that suddenly sprung up around the letters. The divinely beautiful and talented Allana Taranto took my photograph for the back cover. Despite all the demands on her time, Lucy Bartholomy miraculously created the perfect cover. I am indebted to them and the two wonderful men who open this book with their kind words.

And then there were our colleagues at XLibris Press: Cheryl Gratz, publishing consultant, and Rhea Villacarlos, submissions representative.

And behind it all were the indefatigable Sr.Bridget and my equally determined sister in law, Melissa Shoaf, busily selling books that did not even exist. They were a bicoastal force to be reckoned with.

Through it all I have had the unconditional support of two men I hold dear to my heart: Oliver Hill and Mahadev.

Finally, I offer my deep gratitude to the small group at The Boston Home, Eileen Toland, Anne Johansen, Tina Nichols, and Lucille Haratsis, for their part in keeping the conversation going.